MÖTLEY CRÜE

THE OFFICIAL BIOGRAPHY

THE FIRST FIVE YEARS

"This book was written on Quick Brew teabags, lots of Tipp-Ex, Beechams Powders, BIC ballpoints, a Hermes Ambassador typewriter and Wild Women!" A platinum thanks to: Doc McGhee, Doug Thaler, Julie A. Foley and especially the very happenin' Rich 'Fish' Fisher.

Cover photograph by Neil Zlozower; most other pics by Mark Weiss. Other pics courtesy of Ross Halfin/REPFOTO LONDON, and Chris Walter. Whilst every effort has been made to trace and contact the photographers of all the pictures, in some cases it was impossible. The publishers apologise to any photographer who has not been credited.

First published in Great Britain in 1985 by Zomba Books, Zomba House, 165–167 Willesden High Road, London NW10 2SG

© Dante Bonutto, 1985

ISBN 0 946391 72 6

Typeset by Panache Typesetters

Cover Design by **Steve Joule**
Book Design by **Rob Burt**
Printed in Singapore through Print Buyers' Database Ltd

First Edition
Reprinted 1986

MÖTLEY CRÜE

THE OFFICIAL BIOGRAPHY

THE FIRST FIVE YEARS

BY DANTE BONUTTO

ZOMBA BOOKS

Contents

Opposite page: the author getting to know his subject at Donington '84.

The Prölogue

IT'S LATE. All over the city people are pinching out candles and hurrying home; climbing on trains and buses or nosing company cars through a constant stream of other company cars, a fender-to-fender flotilla steaming and swearing its way out into the suburbs. It's the end of the working day; shackles have been shaken and mental slates wiped clean as the good God-fearin' folk of London prepare to rub soothing balm onto noses pressed long and hard against the corporate grindstone.

But not me. It may be dark out in the street but I've got a deadline snapping at my heels and a news page staring back at me clean, crisp … and blank. Once again I must face the moment of truth and I must face it *alone*.

In a way, this is the hardest part of the job; sometimes when you fix your eyes on the cold expanse of the page it's almost like peering unwittingly into the hollower chambers of the soul, a desperate search for solace that ultimately leaves the palms both damp and empty. Sometimes, with the snow-white sheet imprisoned inside the typewriter yet taunting and teasing still, inspiration just isn't enough and the creative juices require a little

gentle foreplay to get them on the move. Sometimes … oh, to hell with all this bullshit, sometimes you just need Mötley Crüe!

If I was asked to supply my single most vivid memory of the Los Angeles four-piece then this would have to be it: sitting alone in the *Kerrang!* magazine office, fingers poised above ancient steam-driven typewriter keys and ear pressed tight to crackling phone receiver, absorbing graphically detailed blow-by-blow accounts of the band's latest exploits. To protect the innocent, my West Coast contact must remain nameless, but there was no question that he had his finger close to the LA pulse, and judging from some of the stories he came up with, pretty much in touch with erogenous quarters too!

Simply, it was impossible for any member of Mötley Crüe to leave their shared apartment without *Kerrang!*'s own roving eye and running nose jotting it down for future reference, and when they squeezed themselves into dead black cow and headed for the clubs (an almost nightly ritual), well then the Hollywood hot-line really *did* start to glow …

'They did what?! And he was dressed as a Marine, you say? Are you SERIOUS?'

It was choice stuff, just the thing to keep both gossip and news pages nicely packed and a definite life-

saver if the week had been a touch on the safe side. Yeah, you could always rely on the Crüe for a decent story, though it was the band's first serious photo session that really set the air alight, in particular a solo snap of fresh-faced vocalist Vince Neil–21 years old and, according to the press hand-out, liable to set 'the girls' hearts throbbing'.

Well, there was no arguing with that; butter certainly wasn't gonna melt in this guy's mouth, but what about his hair? I mean, c'mon! Never before had a top knot so brazenly flaunted all the known laws of science. Was it real? Was it airbrushed? Was the world flat?

To find out the answers to these questions and others besides you'll just have to read on, but my considered advice is not to stray too far from *terra firma* in the meantime. What I can reveal, however, is that our four latter-day mop tops – Nikki Sixx (bass), Tommy 'T-Bone' Lee (drums), Mick Mars (rüde guitar) and the aforementioned Mr Neil (lead vocals) – have now risen to an exalted position as one of the premier heavy rock outfits on the face of this planet (flat or otherwise), trailing broken nights and drunken hearts in their wake.

The look of these 'art-wrecko cherubs', always individual and always shifting, has rubbed off on those in their backyard and beyond, though in terms of attitude and intent they remain remarkably unchanged. A little tidier around the edges perhaps, a little less inclined to the arrogant pose and the flip-off phrase, but still bad boys at heart, constantly hugging the fast lane (complete with occasional tragic twist) in an all-or-nothing bid for ultimate unrepentant glory.

Their third and most ambitious LP *Theatre Of Pain* is now on release, yet Mötley Crüe isn't simply a musical project, more a philosophy, a way of life. All things to all men and a lot more to all women …

'Like breaking over a mountain and seeing a sunset glistening through broken, moisture laden clouds; a rainbow of melody and a power that brings your senses to the outsides of your flesh,' is how publisher Glen Chileski saw things.

'The loudest and grossest band in the history of rock'n'roll,' is Nikki's more succinct view, and being a recognised consultant on all things loud and gross (a genuine gutter-level guru) I guess he really ought to know.

DANTE BONUTTO

Act One
In The Beginning

An early publicity shot—note Nikki's creative use of a telephone cord . . .

'When we first came out everybody was laughing at us 'cos there were these four guys who looked the same, then all of a sudden the audiences started to dress like us, and it grew and grew ...' – Nikki Sixx.

IT'S NOW called Club Hollywood and can be rented out for private parties and movie or video making, but back in May 1981 the site on the corner of Crescent Heights and Santa Monica Boulevard was the home of famed Los Angeles rock club The Starwood, stamping ground for such homespun talent as Quiet Riot and London.

These two groups certainly played there more than most, the former featuring a soon-to-be legend in guitarist Randy Rhoads (tragically killed in a flying accident in Florida whilst a member of the Ozzy Osbourne band) and the latter a skinny shag-topped bassist under the unlikely monicker of Nikki Sixx – a *nom de guerre* 'nikked' perhaps from Jon And The Nightriders' Nikki Syxx, who had used the monicker since the mid '70s. They were what you might call the 'regulars', though on May 24/25, a Sunday/Monday, it was Oakland based Y&T – Yesterday & Today at this point – who had the venue booked, with a local quartet called Mötley Crüe set to support on all four shows (two per night).

Mötley Crüe? The name didn't set off too many bells and let's face it it's not the sort of banner you're likely to forget, though the bassist at least cast an acknowledged silhouette. The skinny frame (about as much meat as a Boxing Day turkey), the shag top (a wild tumescent tuft obliterating sight), the unlikely monicker ... this man was no stranger, but why wasn't he still in London (the band)? And who or what were Mötley Crüe?! The mists were soon to rise ...

Quite simply, this was the first time that Tommy, Mick, Vince and Nikki (for it was he) had played together in public, and not a bad start either. According to local gig lore, a weekend spot at The Starwood – support or otherwise – was certainly something to crow about ('You play those nights, you're God' – Vince), and for a band making its debut appearance, a way of cutting the ribbon and cracking the champagne on a likely looking career, it was truly an impressive move. A genuine coup.

In fact, it was all down to Nikki

and the fact that London, a group he co-founded with guitarist Lizzy Grey, were at one stage managed by David Forest, who also ran The Starwood. Nikki would help clean up there during the day, push a broom and polish glasses, the usual routine, then escape quietly out the back with his hair under a hat, to return later (after a brief twirl in a telephone booth) as Nikki Sixx, local celebrity and star of stage and scream. After enough Jack Daniels and coke, every Mega Hero's choice, he was nudging Superman out of his flight path and taking any multi-storey dwelling in his stride.

On an LA club level, London didn't have to answer to or open for anyone, so when Nikki pieced together a new project the strength of his name and reputation ensured that any strings he chose to pull were dangling at least vaguely close to hand. His new band was ready for inspection and The Starwood seemed the perfect parade ground, so ... in front of a partisan Y&T crowd speckled with a few fellow musicians keen to check out the latest Sixx creation, Mötley Crüe placed stiletto heels on boards for the very first time. Scientists duly reported a slight shift of the world on its axis ...

THE INITIAL, reaction to the troupe, however, was one of acute suspicion, an unspoken consensus to keep a safe bargepole's distance until the four folk on-stage had slipped into *something* approaching a defineable category. The rakish looks, the cock-of-the-walk stance, I mean just *who* did these guys think they were?

Clearly, this was Y&T's public and they weren't going to succumb without a fight. They didn't ...

'There was one guy in the audience who was giving us trouble,' recalls Nikki, 'and when he came on-stage I smashed his face with my bass, Tommy hit him with his drumsticks right between the eyes and Vince slammed him with a flashlight. There was blood on my guitar as we finished the encore. It was great! Right away, people knew this was a band that was going to get respect.'

He was right. The two shows the second night were a different story.

'Oh yeah,' says Vince, 'the second night we had 'em!'

'By the time we played our last set the crowd were going "Yeah!" and when Y&T came back to finish off there must have been no more than eighty people left,' adds Mick, who sensed at this point that after a few years wandering in the wilderness,

Another early promo pic; Nikki's name and reputation helped get the band its first gig at The Starwood.

sleeping in parks with his Les Paul a constant bench-fellow, he had at last discovered the Promised Band ...

'The first set the first night I was going "OK, OK", the second set I was thinking "Wow, this is interesting" and during the second set the second night I went "This is it!"'

Cue the parting of the Red Sea and cheers from a cast of thousands, not to mention an excited, spontaneous rendition of the 'Hallelujah Chorus'. Well, David Forest was humming along anyway ...

'I book ten, maybe twelve bands a week at The Starwood,' he explained at the time, 'and Mötley Crüe's debut was the first occasion in years I've actually watched the *whole* show and was entertained and excited the

whole time. They worked the Starwood audience into a frenzy – their show was a knockout. Every song seems to be hit oriented. I see no reason Mötley Crüe won't make it huge.'

And Mick saw no reason either.

'The kids were ready for something new, I think. After that, things just kept on getting bigger and better ...'

HANG ON a minute though, let's not get carried away here. Mötley Crüe were off and running certainly, but after such a spectacular start their second gig must have been something of a letdown – a fairly low-key affair at Pookie's sandwich and beer shop in Pasadena, just across the street from the site of the old 1700-capacity Perkins Palace. It was a two act set-up, a double-header with a band called Stormer, which might have filled the place (just taking its first tentative steps into the world of showbiz) to its 200 limit … but didn't. On the night, around thirteen people put in an appearance, a remarkably unlucky number for those on-stage who, to their infernal credit, dispensed the 'devil's song' regardless, refusing to temper either musical or alcoholic excess.

For the Crüe, it was a particularly eventful night. Not only did they successfully break the 100 dollar barrier on their bar tab (an achievement subsequently repeated many times, no problem), but a particularly out-to-lunch roadie-cum-space cadet captain also managed to drive away the van before their stage clothes had been unloaded. Hence, the first set of the evening had to be executed in 'civvies' – though Mötley Crüe's off-stage apparel might well be classed as 'drag' by some of rock's more conventional sons – probably the only time this has happened, and certainly the only time *that* night. When the four broke their chains for set number two, they were resplendent in their usual hand-me-

down chic, dressed to carve up and kill, frantically attended by a roadie who appeared to be nursing punctures in all vital organs. It couldn't be, of course, the idea is *way* too far-fetched, but he looked as though he'd been walked over by several pairs of stiletto-heeled boots. Most strange …

A successful outing, then, after a somewhat unexpected start, and Mötley Crüe did indeed go on to play Pookie's again (September 11/12, a Friday/Saturday). Perhaps to revive nostalgic memories? Perhaps to keep firmly in touch with their roots? It's possible, I suppose, though the outstanding bar bill might have had something to do with it too! Still, whatever the reason, laudable or laughable, noble or no-choice, it was already clear to the point of transparency that this new outfit were far more than just another bunch of Van Halen clones. They had something special, something extra–beyond mere hollow legs!

The Crüe had held firm for two gigs; they could now survive anything …
PRETTY MUCH from the squeeze of the trigger, Mötley Crüe had taken on the LA scene as a top-of-the-bill act, heads held high (enabling them

to see 'neath a collective canopy of hair) and backs to the wall (enabling them to stand after a hard night at the Rainbow Bar & Grill, a notorious heavy metal pick-up parlour in West Hollywood). They did play a co-headline show at the 1000-plus-capacity Country Club at Reseda in the Valley with another local outfit called Snow (at this point featuring Carlos Cavaso of Quiet Riot on guitar) going on above them. But for the most part their early appearances were headline ones, in the course of which they packed the LA venues with an ever-growing following, loud of mouth and loyal of heart. There was no way initially hesitant club owners could argue with *them* …

The Troubadour (Saturday June 6 1981), The Starwood (Thursday July 9), The Barn, Alpine Village (Thursday August 6), The Excelsior Auditorium (Saturday August 15), American Bandstand (Friday August 28) and The Troubadour again (Friday September 4), it was here that the Crüe laid the raucous, rabble-rousin' roots for their S.I.N. (Safety In Numbers) fan club, currently taking in some 3000 unrepentant S.I.N.N.E.R.S across the US. For them, receiving an update on

The initial newsletter from the Crue's S.I.N. (Safety In Numbers) fan club. For bad boys (and girls) only . . .

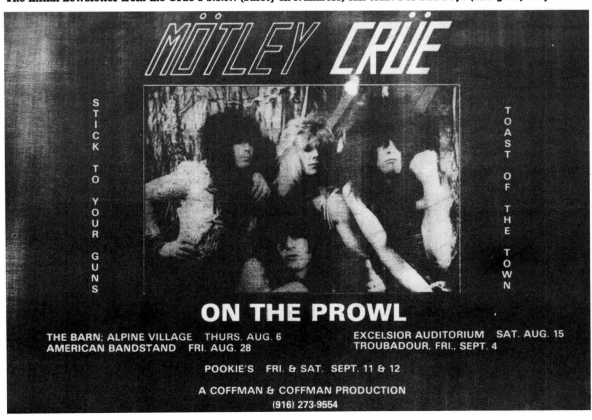

Welcome Sinners To The

MÖTLEY CRÜE

Newsletters #1

Sin Club

The early Crue stage set with home-made drum riser and backdrop. The riser was later sold to LA outfit Ratt.

MC activity every four months in return for a seven dollar contribution to The Caüse (plus, of course, a dollar for postage and handling – even sin ain't free these days!), it's already too late, but none have yet sought out salvation. Sometimes, as Nikki says, 'being a bad guy is definitely more fun ...'

Playing two, sometimes three, sets a night, the band's music was primarily original spiced up with the occasional cover version: The Beatles' 'Helter Skelter' and 'Paperback Writer', and Elvis' 'Jailhouse Rock', the latter mixed together with 'Hound Dog' and 'My Babe' (a number of the '76 *Fool For The City* LP by Savoy Brown breakaway boogie masters Foghat). Later on, they also dabbled with 'Two-timer', a song on Scorpions' drummer Herman Rarebell's '81 solo album *Nip In The Bud*, though in terms of stage-set and costume, they were an *all* original outfit from the off, relying on inspiration and perspiration to an equal complementary degree. Vince and Tommy joined forces to build a drum riser, a two-tier affair housing a number of lights later sold to fellow LA hopefuls Ratt and featuring proudly in their *Round And Round*

video, while a giant sheet ablaze with the Mötley Crüe logo was strung up as a backdrop. As for the stage clothes, well, they were a hotch-potch of anything and everything ...

'We were trying to be larger than life,' says Vince, 'and different from anything else that was out there. We'd cut up T-shirts, go to a hardware store on Santa Monica Boulevard to buy chains and Nikki would sometimes wrap himself up in a phone cord. Anything we could find we would wear; anything a little unusual and still kinda cool ... *rags* even! If we saw something blowing down the middle of the street, we'd stop the car and reach out for it; old newspapers and bags, that kinda stuff. We'd rob the 'bag ladies'. Beat them up,' he chuckles. 'Take all their shit, all their clothes ...'

'It was a growing stage for us: I guess it was our *awkward* stage. Actually, I thought we looked pretty sharp back then, for what we had – which was nothing! We did the best we could and we pulled it off ...'

TO BEGIN with, however, the Crüe's unceasing search for the original and the never before attempted was undermined a little by constant comparisons between Vince and Van Halen frontman Dave Lee Roth, already a good neck ahead in the celebrity stakes. Ol' Diamond Dave gave the four his seal of approval by continuing to air his much lauded features at their gigs, thereby making the link stronger still; indeed, at one Troubadour outing he was even set to join Vince and Co. on-stage for an all-in 'Jailhouse Rock' jam, and no doubt would have done had he not been otherwise disposed when the Big Moment finally came. Ah well, that's showbiz I guess, though gradually the Crüe began to pull apart, staking serious territorial claims and establishing an identity that made it clear even to the most scarlet of necks that, *no*, they weren't gay and, *no*, they weren't anybody's sisters either! Following a brief visit to Los Angeles in late '83, in fact, I came back proclaiming that 'in my opinion (formed after approximately six scotch'n'cokes on the Country Club balcony) the LA look has as much to do with the shaggy tops and chrome'n'leather bottoms of Mötley Crüe as the knotted hankies and wind-assisted hairdo of Dave Lee Roth or (more recently) the 'barber's pole' chic of Quiet Riot ...' (*Kerrang!* 57, December 15-28).

This, admittedly, was a little later down the line, but even much earlier on a Mötley Crüe member was unlikely to be lost in a crowd. A

Vince rubbing shoulders with 'Diamond' Dave Lee Roth. Early in the Crue's career comparisons between the two were constant.

circus or a sci-fi movie perhaps, but drop any one of the four into a convenient sea of humanity and you'd have no trouble singling them out on the surface. This was it, a Smog City 'spider' style (eight legs, lots of hair!) that will now and forever spell Mötley Crüe: the crowning plumes, teased and tormented into upright stance–dyed blue-black in the case of Nikki, Tommy and Mick, white in the case of Vince and all

their own work – the studded hand-pieces, the make-up, the stiletto heels and the quite appalling blue trousers persevered with by Mick (fashioned out of the stuff you 'normally cover couches with' according to Vince), it all added up to what West Coast impressario and professional boaster Kim Fowley considered the 'best international image since Sweet and the best European image since Japan ...'

MÖTLEY CRÜE

STICK TO YOUR GUNS
TOAST OF THE TOWN

With only a thousand ever pressed, a pristine copy of the first Crue single can sell for as much as $500!

It was a definite look, a style more lowdown street than *haute couture*, and certainly not manufactured or premeditated in the way that bands in the 'pop' field often have their image synched in with the trend or fashion of the day in a fleeting front page flourish. No way, nossir! This wasn't about conforming *or* compromise, quite the opposite, in fact. Each member of the group had looked pretty much the same in previous musical existences give or take the odd smear or scarf ('we all stood out in each of our bands: I was the only guy who would 'rat' my hair and wear make-up' – Tommy), and coming on heavy in attitude and image at a time when narrow ties and minds held sway within the industry showed that shoulder to shoulder, heel to heel, the four rebel Crüesters were not prepared to play the record company game. Propped up arrogantly in dim, dusky corners, flashing dagger looks at random, they decided to hold both ground and principles and let the world come to *them*. A noble gesture certainly, though magnanimity is a poor substitute for money when it's the rent man who leads the charge ...

THOUGH SOMETHING of a backlash now appears to have set in, the (Wild) West Coast recently found itself in the full-blooded throes of a genuine metal boom, with loud dress, loud music and anything wrapped in chains or barbed wire getting a bold thumbs-up from the 'Chequebook Charlies' and a slightly more demonic alignment of the fingers from the fans. However, when Mötley Crüe were (literally) getting their act together, the LA rock base was about as sturdy as an iceberg in the Sahara, with the A&R brigade continuing to turn over stones in their search for a Knack Knumber Two when most right-minded folk felt the one they had already was more than sufficient, thank you ...

On the tight-knit club circuit the Crüe were a snowballing success, causing local palpitations alongside Snow, Smile (Mötley faves, as were Satyr and Missing Persons), Yankee Rose and Quiet Riot, yet it took a while for the record companies to stop feeding their noses for a second and take a hard look at what was blossoming right under 'em. Heavy rock just wasn't the flavour of the month – *any* month – and so it wasn't getting supported. Full stop. Which made it tough for the aforementioned acts, and others, to get across to a wider non-West Coast audience.

On some the stress and the frustration took a heavy, damaging toll. Leathers were hung up and Marshalls turned down; people who under normal circumstances could be relied upon to cut their throats before their hair suddenly went ahead and did the dirty deed, making it quite clear that the way of the rocker was under heavy fire and ammunition was low. According to the Mötley Crüe scheme of things, this left just one place to go. *Nowhere*, that well known holiday resort for the impoverished and the immobile. Just bite the last bullet and stick to your guns, appropriately the A-side of the band's first independent single ...

With only a limited number ever made available, this 'Stick To Your Guns'/'Toast Of The Town' release has now become something of a collector's item. Vince reckons he's seen copies on sale for as much as 500 dollars, remarkable when you consider that it was never at any time for sale, simply given away at gigs. Showing the reticent majors a united back view, the band simply upped and formed their own Leäther Records label (a name conjured up in a local Denny's coffee shop), producing the single themselves with engineer Laura Livingston and arranging for 1000 copies to be pressed up. In June '81, after three days in Crystal Sound Studios on Hollywood's Vine Street, the Crüe found themselves juggling one very hot potato indeed.

Mention the record to Nikki today and he'll tell you from behind a wry smile that it sounds 'horrendous, though the songs are good' (he doesn't own a copy), but at the time it served a strictly limited purpose and it served it well. When Vince walked out on-stage wafting a copy back and forth, dispensing the distinctive aroma of the freebie, it encouraged reluctant wall-flowers to extend their roots a little closer to the front. And when he held high the disc in triumph at the end of the show, the hands of the audience automatically went up too. The reaction may have been, shall we say, *encouraged*, but it was the right reaction nonetheless, a way of finally breaking the ice between a shy or shell-shocked crowd and a new, somewhat disorientating act. Forget the method, it was the madness that counted!

'Well, it got a buzz around,' explains Vince, 'cos if you had anything on plastic you were cool. It gave us a bit more status.' (Mr. Neil, incidentally, does own a copy of the record – complete with genuine coffee stain – but isn't open to offers ...).

Act Two
The Grand Design

'I was always in Mötley Crüe but I didn't know it 'till we all met ... I was looking for these individuals who were like I was, with an aggressive attitude towards music, a true bad attitude. When the four of us got together it was like a first!' – Nikki Sixx

'TRANSVESTITE VAMPIRES after a nuclear holocaust', 'leather-bound devil-hookers', occupants of some 'strange sex-fantasy palace, or some Fellinian Theatre of the Apocalypse' ... in their time Mötley Crüe have been called a whole variety of different names, and indeed it's not beyond the realms of possibility that when they first came into contention back in the Summer of '81 it could have been under a vastly different monicker. Christmas, to be precise. And then, of course, there was Trouble, and Bad Blood, and Holiday, and Suicidal Tendencies, all sorts of suggestions ... including Christmas.

Nikki really went for the name – still does, in fact – and may well put it to appropriate use at some future uncharted date, but as for the other three, well, they were less keen. Having nothing to do with reggae, soul or funk they could have amended it to *White* Christmas, I suppose, or reduced personnel by a quarter and become Christmas *Three* but, no, they just weren't buying it. Mick, happily, came to the rescue ...

'Back in '77, I was rehearsing with this group called White Horse,' he explains, 'and we were all just laying around on the floor, y'know. Then the bass player walks in and goes "this certainly is a motley looking crew!" So I wrote it down and that's how the name came about; I spelt it M-O-T-T-L-E-Y K-R-U-E, though ...'

It was perfect. Even ol' Santa Claus Sixx had to admit that, conjuring up exactly the right sort of image. It was messy and sloppy (in the nicest possible way) and generally representative of the band's frame of mind which Nikki, in the absence of sound psychiatric opinion, chooses to define as 'gypsy like'. He tidied it up a touch, of course – though in the great and cherished tradition of Slade a certain degree of artistic licence was maintained – and added the umlauts to instill a sense of the cool and the militant.

'We're into that kind of stuff,' he told Xavier Russell in *Kerrang!* (issue 30, December 2-15 1982), 'everything very organised. The Germans in the early days of the war were extremely militant and that's where I came up with the idea because we were going for a heavy, aggressive *German* heavy metal sound ...'

If the bassist couldn't have Christmas then he wanted a name like AC/DC or Cheap Trick, neither of whom have to fight too hard for space on his stereo. The result: Mötley Crüe. Mick's idea but definitely Nikki's baby. A new band had been born and the screaming and the kicking (ass) were already underway ...

ON A LOCAL Los Angeles level at least, Nikki's previous outfit London certainly enjoyed something approaching celebrity status, though their finely-honed talent for consuming vast and regular quantities of alcohol gave them something of a shady reputation. Perhaps like Jack Russell, vocalist with fellow LA rock-spawn Great White, they'd been forced to eat liver as kids and were now exacting some horrible systematic revenge on their own. Whatever the reason, these were very much home-town boys made *baaaad*.

Nikki co-founded London with guitarist Lizzy Grey (the two combining to write 'Public Enemy # 1', later to appear on the debut Mötley Crüe album), though personnel changes have continued apace since the former jumped ship to start up something new. Lizzy remains, however, augmented now by Bobby Marks on drums (ex-Ratt/Steeler), Brian West on bass (ex-TKO) and Nadir D'Priest on vocals, and the group continues to play the LA circuit, sporting a fresh image and with 'Public Enemy ...' noticeably excluded from the set.

At one time, with Nikki writing 50 per cent of the original material, lyrics included (stuff like 'Radio Star', 'Can't Buy Love' and 'LA Jets'), and former Mott singer Nigel Benjamin spitting out the songs upfront along with the odd Bowie/Mott The Hoople cover, London had no trouble packing 'em in clubs like The Troubadour and sending 'em out smiling, yet somehow a major deal continued to elude them (it still does). The name was OK, capital(!) in fact, clearly displaying the British influence at work, and they seemed to have all the answers: the only trouble was, for one reason or another the record companies consistently declined to pop the

Da Crue's early suggestions for a name included 'Holiday' and 'Christmas!'.

question. Nikki has his own theory on the matter ...

'I really think the band didn't take itself seriously enough,' he explains. 'There were inner feuds and it just wasn't the right time, I guess. The

record companies didn't wanna know. We were like a punk band, y'see, we really couldn't play that well together. I mean, in Mötley Crüe I am definitely the worst musician, though now I've gotten to the stage where my playing, I think, is very, very good. But if you can imagine a bunch of musicians who

were just starting to get their chops together, drank excessively (told you!) and really cared more about the image than the music, then you'll have a fair idea why London didn't get a deal ...'

In those days, Nikki cut roughly the same dash as he does now – a little thinner maybe, though just as

wild – but the rest were more into a New York Dolls type of look; a scuzz-club style 'n' swagger with a pretty-boy polish, (The story of his life) he stood out ...

'The other guys in the band were always going to me "you're too over-the-top, you should calm down a bit", but when I get up on-stage I

'Loud, Rude, Aggressive Guitarist Available' said Mick's ad in the *Recycler*, and he was . . . on all counts!

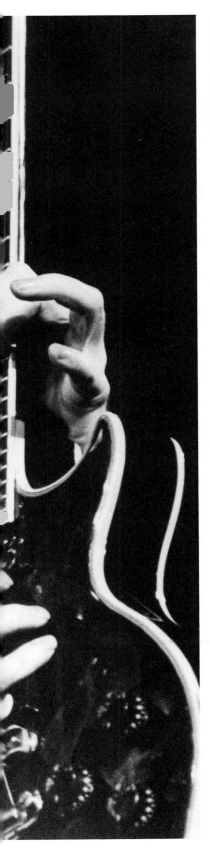

feel the roar of the lion. I almost change personality when I start playing, this really demented side of me comes out. I can't explain it.'

As far as Nikki's concerned, Mötley Crüe is the first *deadly* serious band he's been involved with, though that doesn't mean he regards London as a joke, a personal Spinal Tap. Far from it.

His time with that outfit, and others previously, he views in much the same way as any professional person would their training and tuition and any craftsmen their apprenticeship. London was like going to school: it got him on the right track and pushed him one step closer to realising his dream. Frankenstein? Huh! He had it easy. Nikki, eyes burning and cauldron a-bubble, was looking to create an altogether weightier monster, an unholy midnight fusion of Black Sabbath and Sweet, the blowtorch bluster of 'Paranoid' ruthlessly deflowering the prime pop culture of 'Ballroom Blitz'. Call it unnatural, call it a breach of God's Law, call it Fred if you like, but one thing's for certain: The Aim Remains The Same.

FIRED BY his mission, it eventually became clear to Nikki that what he wanted to do and what the rest of London wanted to do were two parallel lines never drawing any closer. The songs that appeared on the first Mötley Crüe LP were originally destined for this band, but with that old 'musical differences' cloud looming large and black on the horizon, he thought it best to stash them away until sunnier times. Deep, deep down within laced-up leather he felt he should move on, and after an initial meeting with near lookalike Tommy he knew he was right. All change, pleeze ...

He quit the group along with frontman Benjamin, leaving Blackie Lawless (currently with LA hotshots W.A.S.P.) to enter the scene on lead vocals, and set his mind working on something new. Beneath the impenetrable outer casing of hair the cogs began to tick over, grinding out the direction he wanted his new band to take, while Tommy, only seventeen at the time and 'jazzed to be in *any* kind of outfit', surveyed the scene with a good deal of awe. I mean, it's not every day you're asked to form a group by someone whose poster is proudly hanging on your bedroom wall, right?

'When Nikki was in London they always made these big, cool-looking posters whenever they played in town and I had some of those. So when he called me up I just went "you're kiddin', this *can't* be Nikki!" but it was. It seems an old guitar player friend of mine had recommended me and given him the number.'

Up until this point, Tommy had been providing the drive for a power trio called Suite 19, playing alongside guitarist Greg Leon and a bassist who, as far as anyone seems to know, has now left the music biz to work for a newspaper company. According to the drummer, they weren't too bad at all, slotting neatly into the UFO groove and gaining support slots with the old Quiet Riot (at The Starwood, inevitably) and Y&T. They did alright, but lacking hard-nosed professional instincts eventually fell by the wayside, leaving Tommy out on a limb and Nikki with a potential first recruit ...

'Actually, the first time I went over to his house the guy scared the shit outta me!' recalls Tommy with a grin. 'He was just sitting there with his hair in his eyes (as always!), and then he goes "what do you think about forming a band?" He was scarey: it was really weird meeting the guy.'

With Tommy duly sworn into the ranks of this unnamed project, the two of them started rehearsing with a guitarist in the front room of the small house in North Hollywood, where Nikki was living at the time. Things went OK, then the idea arose that maybe the band should have *two* guitarists, the old rhythm'n'lead double act, so response was made to an ad in the *Recycler* (a general paper read by musicians) that particularly caught their eye. It said, quite simply: 'Loud, Rude, Aggressive Guitarist Available', going on to mention vocal capabilities and giving a name and phone number. The number I can't tell you, but the name's no problem ... it was Mick.

THE FACT that the ad was there in the first place wasn't particularly unusual; a lot of guitar players, indeed players in general, choose to promote themselves this way while 'resting' between bands, it's standard practice. You know the kind of thing: 'RED HOT GUITARIST AVAILABLE', 'HOTTEST GUITAR PLAYER IN THE WORLD AVAILABLE', 'FRETS BURNT BY APPOINTMENT', wildly extravagant and blatantly bogus, the sort of stuff that makes you think Hendrix isn't really dead, just pushing for a gig. Mick, teed off with all this nonsense, decided to go for the more honest approach. He *couldn't* play guitar while hanging upside down with his

**The Crue about to show a modest
and retiring follower exactly
what goes where.**

hair on fire and both hands tied to
rampant shire horses, but he *was*
loud, rude and aggressive – on a
good day! He laid his cards face up
on the table and got a good
response; even Sparks called him
up, 'but I told 'em on the phone that I
was into a different type of music to
what they were doing and we'd just
be wasting each others time. They
said, "thanks for being so honest …"'

Having been weaned on heavy
rock, in particular Mountain
(featuring guitarist Leslie West), Jimi
Hendrix, early Jimmy Page, Jeff
Beck and old Deep Purple, he just
wasn't prepared to compromise
ideals at this stage of his career.
When Nikki and Tommy rang
his bell, he knew he wouldn't have

to …

'They asked me what kind of
equipment I had and what I looked
like: I told 'em I had blue-black hair
down to the middle of my back and
they went "oh, you use Nice'N'Easy
(a hair dye) too, huh?!" '

Clearly, fate was lending a
hand …
ACTUALLY, MICK had met up with
Nikki some three years earlier,
before the latter was even in London.
At that point, the bassist had a job in
a local liquor store (probably to be
close to Jack Daniels 'my best friend
in the world!') and the guitarist, sad
to say, *was* compromising ideals,
playing down the street in, of all
things, a cowboy band!

'I invited Nikki to come down and
see me,' recalls Mick, 'and we sat
there and got drunk together and I
played guitar. I think he was
impressed because in those days I

was heavily into slide and I would
make use of the mikestand just to be
different.'

There was vague talk of the two
collaborating on some material, the
usual thing musicians discuss when
the hour's late and the bottle's empty,
but Mick was going through a
second divorce at the time and was
more or less homeless, just making
the best of things in a garage with
his ex-brother-in-law. The best laid
plans and all that, and the next time
the pair came haircut to haircut was
when Mick went along to audition
for this new burgeoning project with
the tentative seasonal title.

'Y'know, when we opened the
door to Mick we didn't even have to
hear him play,' says Tommy. 'We
went "*this* is the guy, he's disgustin'!" '

'Yeah, I thought he was terrible
looking,' adds Nikki laughing, 'it was
great! He was a real sinister

character, like a reject from the Addams Family, which is just what I wanted. His shoes were taped together and he had a jacket that was almost falling off him; he simply didn't have a penny to his name, none of us did ...'

'We just sat down and one of the first songs we wrote was 'Stick To Your Guns' and there was an old Raspberries number that we did as well. Then I started showing them *my* songs and it all fell into place. We did ten numbers on that first day and we all went "God, this sounds like magic!" '

Mick, who arrived complete with massive Marshall stacks, well remembers this initial sounding-out session too. Nikki told him he was free to do whatever he wanted with the songs so 'I put some different parts to 'em and Tommy and Nikki were shouting encouragement at me ('We were going "yeah! yeah! YEAH!!", he just blew smoke' – Tommy). They originally had another guitar player there as well and he was pretty good but young and lacking any real finesse so *I* had to fire him ...'

At this formative pre-Vince stage, the band also had a different singer who got to the point of laying something down (never used) but clearly wasn't cutting it, being, according to the ever blunt Nikki, 'a mess all over!' and, in the words of the even blunter Mick, 'at least fifty pounds overweight – I didn't dig that guy ...' Hence, the latter once again took it upon himself to don dark glasses, turn up lapels and live up to the promise of his ad. He may not be a man of many words, but around this period in time most of them appeared to be 'goodbye' (or fairly unsubtle variations thereof).

'Yeah, I had to play the jerk again,' he confesses wearily. 'I called up Nikki and Tommy and said "look, I don't think this guy's gonna work out". '

He was right.

AT WHICH point The Starwood once again weaves back into the action. For it was here, one fateful Tuesday night, that Nikki, Tommy and Mick found the man they wanted to front them: Rock Candy vocalist (cue fanfare) Vincent Neil. Peering back, of course, the choice seems an obvious one, but as with so many discoveries of note it was all down to chance and the omnipresent historical impulse to get well and truly 'rotted' ...

The three, it appears, had gone down to The Starwood for a number of reasons; *a* to check out the Rock Candy guitarist whose goofy Rick

Nielsenesque posturing was apparently well worth a glance, and *b c d e f & g* to take a drink and socialise. There seemed a vague feeling in the camp that a rhythm guitarist might be worth considering, but with Mick not doing lunar somersaults at the idea, all eyes swiftly turned towards the barrel-of-fun blond belting out Sweet and Cheap Trick covers with

a skilled, controlled vengeance. Now and then an original song would creep stealthily into the set, but with the guitarist clearly something of a Cheap Trick fanatic the band relied on that source more than any other to flesh out the bones of their repertoire.

Vince quit Rock Candy to link up with the Crue.

All in all, they had about twenty CT standards to pick'n'choose from, mixing them with Sweet's 'AC/DC', 'Set Me Free' and the like, in a potent party punch with strong ice-breaking potential. It was all good fun in a limited kind of way, a simple reflective background against which Vince could switch on and shine. On this particular evening, he positively glowed...

'His band was terrible, really *bad*', recalls Nikki, who was going through a serious Cheap Trick phase himself at the time, amazed by the arrangements on the *In Color* and *Dream Police* LPs, 'but Vince was in a different class. He just stuck out.'

Mick too was impressed...

'I said "*that's* the guy to front the band right there!" I was really drunk at the time but I went "look, I don't care if he sings flat or if he's off-key; he looks good and he moves well onstage". When we got him down to an audition, though, it just so happened that he *did* sing good.'

Ah, if only it had been that easy! After the show, Nikki and Tommy

The Crue give centrefold-type attention to a full page, full colour pic of themselves in *Kerrang!* **issue 12 (March 25–April 7, 1982).**

cornered the startled Vince in the bathroom away from prying eyes and gave him the whole deal straight from the hip. They were starting up a new band and did he want in? Yes? YES?! Well, you'd have thought that would have been his answer, anyway. True, he didn't know Mick from a can of peaches but Tommy was certainly a friendly grinning face, the two having gone to school together – or, more accurately, *not* gone to school together, pursuing an extra-curricular course in advanced Aerosmith rather than twitch and fidget in the nether reaches of the class. God, they'd even played a few parties together in an unstamped loose alliance, they were far from strangers.

And then, of course, there was Nikki. Vince had never met him before but was certainly conversant with his reputation and name (both a little fabricated, I suspect), which alone might have been enough to make this poaching expedition a success. Frankly, it looked like an offer he couldn't refuse ... he did.

The truth of the matter is that Vince was more than a touch confused; flattered by the offer for sure, yet uncertain which way to jump. Should he stay or should he go? It was difficult to decide ...

'The thing is' he explains, 'I'd just played The Starwood and to me that was a big gig. Why leave something I thought was happenin' to join these guys who hadn't played a gig yet, y'know? So although Tommy dropped off a tape for me to listen to, I stood up the audition.'

'The next night, however, Rock Candy had arranged to play at a party but, with the exception of the drummer and myself, none of the band showed up. All these people were there and there was no band! I didn't know where the other guys were, though I found out later that they'd gone off to some lightweight recording session. Then the next day I heard that Mötley Crüe had found themselves a singer ... I was kicking myself in the butt, going "God, I should have done that!" 'cos the night before I quit Rock Candy for good.'

With their prime target standing them up, the Crüe went on to audition several different singers but didn't strike gold – 'There was just no magic,' sighs Nikki. The result was a swift phone call to Vince who, hampered only slightly by a freshly battered butt, jumped at the prospect of a second saving shot. He met up with the band at Crystal Sound Studios where they were in

the process of recording their first demo tape (Nikki called in an old favour to get the studio time) and instantly turned both hand and tonsils to the 'Stick To Your Guns'/ 'Toast Of The Town' pairing, already earmarked for giveaway release.

He didn't really know the arrangements or the lyrics – in fact, if you listen to the record hard enough you can hear him turning over pages! – but the words to 'Stick To Your Guns' struck a deep personal chord and meant quite a lot to the rest of the group too. 'Get a

grip on yourself/Get in shape for tonight/Take a look at yourself/Are your dreams losing sight?' squealed Vince, clenching a fist in honour of those everywhere who weren't prepared to compromise their vision and making it patently clear that, on a particularly fervent level, Mötley Crüe were four of them.

Out of fashion, out of money and (occasionally) out of it, they simply refused to let others dictate the pace or make up the rules; while the weak rushed to the fire unable to last out in the cold, four hardened survivors

Vince refused to cut his hair when all around were losing theirs (right). Back of the 'Stick To Your Guns'/'Toast Of The Town' single sleeve.

simply dug heels into ice and refused to give their ground. As for the Rock Candy guitarist, well he proved a little easier to budge. Originally a real roots rocker with the stare and stance down pat, he suddenly got the notion that if he shortened his hair and lightened up his attitude he might get Dame Fortune to cut out the winks and wiggles and finally come across.

'So he cut his hair and changed his style and I *didn't'* says Vince, who decided that very night to throw in his lot with the Crüe, assisting in the demolition of some five bottles of Schnapps shared toast for toast and measure for measure with another new recruit, Allan Coffman. All at once, the band had themselves a singer *and* a manager, the latter paying for the record to be pressed and put into sleeves. Check out the back of the single bag and you'll find his elaborate 'Coffman & Coffman' credit – something that was to appear on all Crüe product for a good time to come – and the individual snapshots of the group are also significant, constituting the first MC photo session, serious or otherwise.

Really, it was all pretty ad hoc; a few black and whites rattled off quickly in the hallway of the studio with Vince doing his best to disguise a fast-spreading black eye, the aftermath of an excited night on the town. These days, an attentive make-up artist could make it disappear with barely a flick of the wrist, but back in '81 that sort of extra just didn't fit the budget. No, there had to be an easier (and cheaper) answer, and there was. Acting under Nikki's artistic guidance, Vince simply deposited his hair roguishly over his eyes, thereby increasing animal allure and obliterating the offending shiner. Brilliant, and oh so simple – amazing how Schnapps can lubricate the brain, dontcha think?! Another five bottles, please . . .

Act Three
The Children Of The Beast, God Bless 'em!

'I was different, I was always a dreamer – dreaming about rock music. All I ever wanted to do was play in a rock'n'roll band, though I never wanted to be a rock star and still don't ...'

MORE THAN any other member of Mötley Crüe, Nikki Sixx embraces the twin themes of comedy and tragedy. Out on the road, bereft of responsibility and prey to temptation, no-one has made a more serious study of the art of falling apart and picking up the pieces. When Nikki hits town you can bet that the red paint-brush will be as high and as bright as the Olympian flame and that any candles found protruding from his person will be seriously scalded at all available ends. An unrepentant 'rock pig' (a Floydian slip?), when it's time to party down he has the ability to dig deep, yet when it's time to get on with business he can clear his mind of sundries and concentrate on the job at hand. At labour or lesiure, work or play, he's a true professional with true professional pride ...

'I feel that what we do on-stage is more important than anything else in the world,' he explains, 'but what we do off-stage is up to us. It's nobody's business but our own. If I want to tear a hotel apart and burn it to the ground that's my trip; and if I want to sit in my room alone and read a book that's my trip too. You don't have to be wild and crazy twenty-four hours a day. Any band who says they're insane *all* the time are only fooling themselves – they're gonna burn up! Besides, it's nobody's right to get up on-stage screwed out of their minds, laugh at the kids and then walk away with the money ...'

BORN IN San José, California, twenty-six years ago, Nikki lived with his grandparents (on his mother's side) for quite a few years as his parents were musicians and constantly on the move. His mother, a farm girl from Idaho, divorced his Sicilian father and married the trumpet player in Frank Sinatra's band with which she herself was a back-up singer. They lived a nomadic lifestyle which has inevitably rubbed off on Nikki (at

Nikki: 'On the road I have my guitar and my women and that's all I need.'

one time he was in no city or state for more than six months), though with his grandparents scratching a living from the land, his freewheeling spirit has always been tempered by a certain degree of down-to-earthness. 'My heart's in the country, my feet are in the city with you' is a line from 'City Boy Blues' on the *Theatre Of Pain* LP and it sums up this balance perfectly, Nikki feeling equally at home in either setting – though *home* isn't perhaps quite the right word.

Indeed, early in his life he must have felt a little like an extra in *The Ten Commandments* movie, forever doomed to wander in search of a taste of milk and honey and a low rent apartment in some downtown desert. He travelled with his parents and he travelled with his grand-parents, who were very poor and constantly having to move on to survive ...

'Now it's very uncomfortable for me to stay in any one place,' he explains. 'Maybe later on I'll enjoy it but right at this moment I like being on the road. When a tour ends I get really upset 'cos I know I'm gonna have to go home – to nothing! On the road I have my guitar and my women and that's all I need; I enjoy meeting new people every day.'

Scholastically speaking, Nikki's was very much a case of education on the run. School daze indeed, though 'I was good in class if I wanted to be. If I took the trouble I'd get A's and B's, but if I wasn't interested I'd flunk; just hang out in the hallway trying to think of reasons not to go into the classroom. I was terrible at maths but good at history ... I guess I was always interested in culture.'

Sometimes Nikki is prone to be a

little over-reflective, particularly when what's on his mind is music. That subject he takes *very* seriously – he writes most of the band's songs, including lyrics (many of which are now stored on an IBM Computer at his house) – and he often wishes others would too.

'Y'know, people always ask me about my hair and the costumes ... they say "hey, it was a really wild show!" To which I go "Yeah, I know it was wild, but did you take anything in? Did you learn anything from what I had to say?" '

Perhaps that's expecting a little *too* much – this is rock'n'roll, after all – but then Nikki's always been a man of extremes, pushing himself right to the brink and settling for nothing half-baked or half-hearted. If he can't go all the way then he'd rather not make the trip ...

'I have a lot of energy and there's a lot of things I aim to do,' he explains. 'I don't want to sit in my house and snort cocaine and shoot up heroin and die. I want to create music and do things in this life 'cos God knows you only live so long, no-one gets *out* of life, y'know ...'

'Last year it just started to sink in that this is bigger than all of us, and that's when I realised that I *have* to keep my feet on the ground, I have to be more than nice to everybody around me and I have to remember the word love. That's very important in life, loving people and treating people good. Rock stars are automatically thought of as dirty, lowdown, scummy personalities, but I don't want to be thought of in that way ...'

'When I was thirteen I had certain goals but they're not the goals I have today. I've reached those original goals and now I want to do other things as well. I want to produce and I want to get into writing music for films; I want to try my hand at acting and I want to direct videos; I'm also working on my own book of words 'cos lyrics are my love – I'm really into painting pictures with them, I've spent a lot of hours over the last five years just concentrating on that – and at some point I'd like to collaborate with other artists; that kind of stuff ...'

There was a time when Nikki didn't reckon on sticking around much past forty (live fast, die fast, you know the score), but now his plans extend at least a little further ahead. Good news for music lovers certainly, though if he really expects a long life he would do well to improve his driving technique and, more importantly, stop blowing his nose on serviettes; take it from me, if an enraged restaurant owner doesn't swing for him one day his long-suffering girlfriend certainly will!

BY THE time he was eleven years old Nikki had become both brash and belligerent, channelling a lot of pent-up aggression into football and athletics. When he was told to cut his hair he simply stamped a petulant foot and proclaimed to the world that he wouldn't, though had he been told *not* to cut it he'd probably have plumped for a 'Kojak special' and had his eyebrows trimmed back to match. In other words, his *own* actually, he suddenly became a 'real rebellious little bastard, always stealing things. I used to steal cars with my friends ...'

He also told Marc Shapiro in *Hit Parader* magazine (January 1983) that he could 'get away with anything and not get caught. I admit I was a real juvenile delinquent, but when I was growing up I really didn't feel there was anything else for me to be.'

The upshot of all this was a despairing free transfer, with Nikki leaving his grandparents in Idaho to stay with his mother in Seattle. His track record was far from spotless and it was hoped that the move would nudge him swiftly back into line. Well, that was the theory; the practice, however, proved somewhat different with the sassy youngster being bounced back and forth between parents and grandparents and eventually escaping from home to set up base, intermittently at least, in the juvenile guest wing of a Seattle jail. It was the start of a long and serious association with bars – of one sort or another ...

'At this point, I really got into being a street punk', he recalls, 'I lived on the street and I lived with hookers in whorehouses. I got into selling drugs too. From having a very basic, poor upbringing I suddenly developed this real sinister "I want to play rock'n'roll and *nothing's* gonna stop me" attitude ...'

No great surprise really, as from an early age Nikki had shown both a keen ear for music and a swelling desire to perform. Between the ages of six and nine, living in El Paso, Texas, with his grandparents and also on a ranch in New Anthony, Mexico, his particular party piece was to make up nursery rhymes and get all his cousins and everybody in his class at school to sing along, which – on a more sophisticated level, of course – is what he's still doing today; still getting people to clap to the beat, still getting them to

Nikki points to a naked woman out of shot (honest!) ...

hum along to his lyrics and still getting them to turn up the radio whenever a Mötley anthem rides in on the airwaves. Certainly, that's how he got into music ...

'I guess the first record that ever really hooked me was Jimmy Dean's 'Big Bad John'. That was just about the heaviest thing on the country & western station that my grandparents used to listen to. That got me turned on, so I'd take the guitar and figure out how to play it. Then I got into rock ...'

'My uncle, Don Zimmerman, is the president of Capitol Records in Los Angeles, so they'd send me across these tapes – the Beatles' catalogue, for example. I really liked 'Back In The USSR', I'd listen to the beginning of that over and over again, and 'Helter Skelter' the same; I really went for the heavier stuff which got me into Deep Purple and Black Sabbath and early David Bowie and T. Rex and even early Kiss, which in turn led me to Aerosmith. I always liked the heaviest of whatever it was.'

AT THE tender age of fourteen Nikki took the next logical step; he was asked to pitch in with a band in Seattle and instantly accepted the offer. This was it. Bright lights beckoned and fame wagged a

finger at him from around a nearby corner. He had it all. The ambition, the drive, the will to succeed, the lot. Everything, in fact, except a guitar; a minor detail ...

'The guy who approached me suggested that I meet him at his house the following afternoon, so I said "OK!", borrowed an empty guitar case from somebody and went to Music West, a music store where I used to go every day and practice for four hours on this one guitar, a gold-top Les Paul. When I got inside the store I asked for an application form for work, stuck the guitar in the empty case while the guy's back was turned and closed it; then, when the guy turned round and handed me the form, I said "thank you very much, I'll bring it back tomorrow" and ran off with the price tag hanging out of the case. I went straight over to the other guy's house and said "here I am, ready to play!" '

And he's been at it ever since ...

At first, Nikki's bands were punk outfits ('but punk meaning Aerosmith') ... Pizazz, Baby Jane, just small-time stuff that never took him beyond Seattle, and it wasn't until he packed up and moved to Los Angeles, the Big Smog, that early dreams and ambitions started to appear as more than just the dalliances of a runaway teenage mind. And the reason for the location shift? Well, according to Nikki, it all started with two ounces of mescalin, four lids of pot and the Rolling Stones ...

'I was at a Stones' concert at the Coliseum in Seattle selling drugs on the street to survive and I got busted. I was supposed to appear in court on a possession charge but I escaped to my grandparents' farm in Idaho. I worked the summer shifting bales of hay and moving irrigation pipes, saved up my money and caught a bus to Los Angeles where I bummed a place to stay from my aunt and uncle for four or five months.'

Like so many others before him, Nikki had come to the 'City of Angels' with stars in his eyes and a bigger jangle in his heart than in his pockets. He'd lived with his mother and stepfather in Mexico for a year but things hadn't really worked out, and with his *real* father making it quite clear that he didn't want anything to do with him, no way, he eventually struck out on a solo voyage. A loner all, uh, alone. It was time to sink or swim ...

'To make it in Hollywood you've gotta have big steel balls!' – Arthur Kane, former New York Doll.

ARTHUR KANE *didn't* make it in Hollywood – he gave it his best shot, eventually withdrawing gracefully to the US East Coast – but in the blink of an eye and the punch of a bus ticket there was someone else poised an' ready to fill his footwear. It is said that every thirteen seconds a teenage girl arrives in Hollywood, searching for a dream and the chance to bang a star into the sidewalk, yet inside six months most of them will have given up the chase. To survive in this land of orphans – a candy-floss oasis housing around eighty per cent of all the Rolls Royces ever made – you have to live by your wits and you have to live for today, swerving smartly round the pitfalls, pills and paranoia. Nikki, equipment suitably galvanized, pinched tight his nose and dived straight in...

His first tentative musical steps were as a bass player in a couple of 'Top 40' outfits, having switched instruments two days after he 'borrowed' that first guitar ('I *needed* the power of the bass'), but he didn't really feel happy within such a tight framework, already having a style that was all his own. The Sixx lixx if you like. Dogged to the bone, however, he just kept on writing, kept on learning and, above all, *kept on*; Bad Company, The Babys and the inevitable Cheap Trick, he covered material by them all, and if (or, more accurately, *when*) a band crumbled to pieces around him, he simply moved on to something new, putting everything into his music...

Once away from his aunt and uncle, he lived in 'little dingy places, people's garages and stuff' and took on a succession of dead-end jobs to maintain that vital link between body and soul. At one stage, he was working in a factory from six in the morning to six at night then doing an eight to midnight shift in a liquor store, livening up the evening with an ingenious (thought unfortunately illegal) system of wealth redistribution; there was a lot of money in the till and he didn't have any so it only seemed right to even up the balance. Well...

'I was sleeping in a garage at the time with just a little heater,' he recalls,' I didn't take my money and buy apartments and cars, all I wanted to do was play my guitar and get better amps and equipment.'

At another of his Hollywood haunts, however, the heater became a trifle superfluous with half the building falling victim to a raging blaze. He shared the place with about ten other musicians from a whole cross-section of bands and somebody, it seems, had left something burning. Ah well, Nikki's memories of Chez Charcoal remain fond nonetheless as it was here that he pulled off one of the most successful business strokes ever, getting 200 dollars for a piano rented by a fellow dweller and managing to convince the police that he was totally innocent. 'What *me* officer?! Come on!' Later dealings with the long and fisted arm of the law would prove a little less painless, I'm afraid, but this time around he came out unscathed and on top.

FOR A while, Nikki threw in his lot with Sister, an infamous LA outfit featuring Blackie Lawless and current W.A.S.P. colleague guitarist Chris Holmes; coming on strong with pentagrams and bizarre worm-eating antics they certainly got themselves noticed, but by the time Nikki entered the scene forbidding cracks were already starting to appear. In fact, he never even made it onto a stage with the band and it wasn't until his London era that a few burs of fame finally began to stick to his pants.

Today, of course, he's a platinum-tinged success, occupying a position somewhere between 'famous' and 'infamous' in the Rock'n'Roll Hall Of Fame and, in off duty hours, a comfortable home tucked discreetly into the dark side of the Hollywood Hills. He regularly receives offers to appear in this or that TV show and his face has grinned/growled out from the cover of almost every mag that is (including the UK-based *Publisher,* April '85!), which must be very satisfying considering that not too long ago he was having to work telephone sales jobs to help keep the band a going concern. He's stuck firm in the saddle and that mean, contankerous ol' critter the Hollywood bronco is now well and truly broken, though without the support of his grandparents he might well have ended up prone in the dust...

'Oh yeah, they're really beautiful people,' he says, hand hovering close to heart,' I would do *anything* for them. I would be sleeping in the back of somebody's car and I'd call them collect from a phone booth and they'd say "you can come home or you can stay and pursue your dreams." So I knew that I could always leave, I didn't *have* to stay out on the streets... but I did, because that was my love...'

. . . and details the credentials of the one who got away!

Vince Neil

'I always wanted to be a guitar player more than a singer, but I just wasn't talented enough at it. There's only so many times you can play the theme song to *Bonanza* . . .'

VINCE NEIL may not possess one of rock's most formidable falsettos and as far as 'doormat chests' go he's well and truly stuck in the starting blocks, but put him on a stage–*any* stage, *anywhere*–and the man knows what he's doing.

'That's always come easy for me,' explains the winner of the 'Best Male Vocalist' section of *Circus* magazine's '84 Readers' Poll, 'you lose all your inhibitions on-stage, you don't think about it, you just *do* it', though in quieter moments, away from the outstretched fingers where the follow-spots can't follow, you could probably call him a little on the shy side. As a rule, he prefers to watch TV rather than throw the set out of the window, little things like that, and when he ventures outside his neat'n'tidy apartment in Redondo Beach, California, perhaps to slap a personal star rating on some new junk food emporium (he's something of a 'crap cuisine' connoisseur, citing a 'quarter pounder with cheese, large fries and a coke' as his ideal meal), that distinctive blond mane is often tucked discreetly under a hat. Not a Crüe hard hat, sadly – the protective head-gear pioneered by the 24 year old Vince in the days when the Mötley stageshow involved the artistic use of a chainsaw and several dozen blood capsules – though there has been idle talk of it coming back onto the scene . . .

And speaking of chainsaws, it's no particular secret that the one-time beach (or should that be *bleach*?) boy takes a double squirt of ketchup on more than just his fries, being a longstanding devotee of the 'hack'n' slash' school of film-making. There's nothing to match a good gore movie as far as Vince is concerned, though 'horror films are great too. I like the old ones–the *real* old ones,' he told Jeff Tamarkin in *Circus* magazine, 'like five-in-the-morning movies on the all-night TV stations . . . one of my favourite movies of all time is *The Texas Chainsaw Massacre*–I recorded the movie, and when I'm home I watch it all the time. Also

Night Of The Living Dead . . . I have to keep the lights on, though it gets really intense for me when I'm watching a good horror movie . . .'

THE ONLY LA native in the Crüe camp, Vince was born and bred in Hollywood, right across the street from the race track, and sent off to school in the San Gabriel Valley, meeting up with Tommy in his middle teens. Vince was at Charter Oak High School and Tommy, younger by one year, at Royal Oak, the pair bumping into each other at different parties and forming a firm friendship despite being in rival bands.

'Actually, the outfit that Tommy was in was real wimpy,' laughs Vince. 'They had this chick who played keyboards and they all wore satin vests and stuff–Tommy just stuck out! Anyway, I got kicked out of Charter Oak in my first year and enrolled at Royal Oak . . .'

Why?

'I never went!'

OK.

' . . .and after that me and Tommy just hung out all the time.'

Nothing wrong with that, of course, though not too much of this 'Hanging out' occurred in the vicinity of the classroom, Vince neglecting the 'reading' and 'riting' side to concentrate fully on the 'running away'. He was a consummate baseball player–the only freshman to make the varsity team, in fact–but when it was spelt out to him that a long life on the team equalled short hair on the head, baseball was the inevitable loser. Instead, he turned his attention to impromptu, energetic jam sessions with the similarly enthusiastic Tommy, the set-up being simplicity itself . . .

Vince was on palm-slapping terms with some guys at a nearby warehouse owned by a lightweight PA hire company and, in return for helping them clean up the premises and build the odd thing, they allowed him and his friend a room to rehearse in. Here, unrepentant exiles from the world of the dusty book, the two Crüesters-to-be could wallow wholeheartedly in a mutual love of Aerosmith, indulging themselves as and when they saw fit. 'Train Kept A Rollin'' was an obvious rehearsal fave, as was 'Rock & Roll Part II', the old Gary Glitter anthem covered a couple of years back by Rick Derringer and Carmine

Appice under the guise of DNA. Though he's yet to hear the original (and best) version, Tommy would some day like the Crüe to follow suit.

Altogether now: 'ROCK'N'ROLL, yea-AAHHH, ROCK'N'ROLL!!!'
UP TO the age of ten Vince supported his dreams of eventual Guitar Herodom with regular lessons. He had the basic requirements–an acoustic, a cheap electric ('It didn't even have a brand name!') and a full set of fingers–yet somehow he didn't feel comfortable. Too often when he threw shapes people threw them back, which led him to the conclusion that he'd probably fare better projecting himself more directly. It was a turning point. Soon he was stunning audiences several thousand strong with nothing more lethal than a plastic comb and a well-practised pout. Oh yes . . .

'I remember that before I was in a band I had this little Fender amp which I'd hook up to the radio and just crank with the windows open when my parents weren't at home. You know the Aerosmith song 'Walk This way'? Well, when that came on I'd strut across the room with a comb or something in my hand and make believe that I was Steven Tyler singing to all these people!'

Certainly, a novel variation on the tennis racket or broom handle traditionally employed by phantom JoePerrys, and for a truly authentic simulation of the Tyler technique Vince would, of course, ensure that he fell over the corner of his bed at least twice during the number . . .

Out of the saddle again!
AT THIS point Vince's other great love in life was surfing. It's been well over a year now since he last balanced on a board, but at High School he was one of the hard core, discussing 'peaks', 'troughs' and 'tunnels' with the best and constantly tipping sand out of his shoes . . .

'I used to go on surfing weekends to this place near San Diego,' he recalls, 'to these cliffs near the nuclear power plant they have down there, by a marine base. I'd go there and just sleep on the sand; we'd pack all our stuff into vans, get a bunch of chicks and *ball!*'

'There were different groups of people at school, y'see, different peer groups, and you had to belong to one of them. You either hung out at the park all day and got stoned on pot, or you were in the football or basketball team, or you went surfing all the time. As a guy, you *had* to do one of those things . . .'

Or stomp around in your bedroom, of course. That the young

An ex-hardcore surfer, Vince owes his start to a plastic comb and a well-practised pout.

Vince successfully elevated to an art, being somewhat indifferent about going out to concerts. Sure, a really *big* show might lure him into the open–he fondly remembers seeing ZZ Top and Aerosmiths at Anaheim Stadium on the former's 'Taking Texas To The People' tour, the one where they had cattle, buffalo and snakes on a Texas-shaped stage!–but for the most part he preferred listening to records at home, or better still bashing it out himself in his own front room.

Vince's parents weren't entirely convinced that he would ever see an honest dollar from this whole rock'n'roll business but, perhaps

working on the grossly misguided assumption that it was only a passing phase, something he needed to get out of his system, they didn't raise too many protests if he brought home his cronies to rehearse, placing the living room under strictest *Marshall* law . . .

'They were really cool about the whole thing,' says Vince. 'I remember one time they went out for the night, it was a Friday, so I organised this party. We set up by the pool in the backyard and about

400 people showed up. When my parents got home there were kids on the roof and in the pool and we were playing away–in fact, that was the first time I ever sang in front of anybody–but they didn't get pissed of; they dug it, hung out . . .'

By eighteen Vince was fronting his first serious band, Rock Candy, providing the music at parties and learning his particular craft the only way you can–by getting up there in the firing line and spitting back the ammo. RC did once manage a support gig at Gazarri's, but more often than not they'd be packing up to a thousand High School kids into somebody or other's backyard, building up a reputation as *the* party outfit in the San Gabriel Valley. Wherever beer was drunk straight from the keg, wherever moral virtue was in short supply and whenever getting up tomorrow didn't seem

half as important as getting down tonight, *that's* where Rock Candy stacked their gear.

Says Vince: 'We would find someone and say, "Hey man, can we play at your house tonight and have a party?" They'd go "Yeah, sure!" Then we'd charge two dollars a person to get in. We'd make all the money and these people's backyards would be absolutely destroyed!' (*Scene*, January 26-February 1 1984) VINCE CHOSE not to finish High School, finally confirming with his body what his mind had long known, and started looking around for work. But what? His first real profit-making exercise had been delivering pizza when he was sixteen, but he didn't much fancy a return to that. Too ethnic, perhaps. His father works for the LA County, mechanical division, taking care of the Sheriffs' cars, but that wasn't quite his bag either. No, he was after something more constructive, like . . . like . . . like building freeway bridges. Well, it's certainly *constructive* if a touch hard on the back . . .

'Oh yeah, we're talkin' hard labour here,' he groans. 'I thought: I need something easier. I was living with this girl at the time and her dad / owned an electrical company, so he took me on. I started off just digging ditches (also not too kind on the back) but I ended up able to wire a whole place by myself, and I still like to get my hands dirty sometimes. If Mötley Crüe hadn't made it, I'd probably be an electrician now; it's a good trade.'

There's no doubt that his colleagues at work seemed friendly enough, helping him move equipment to gigs despite the fact he couldn't pay them. He liked the job and it taught him a lot, but he'd certainly be giving his butt another serious seeing-to if the closest he came to the rock'n'roll lifestyle today was sitting at home listening to his favourite LP – *Lovedrive* by the Scorpions – or, worse still, down by the skirting board fitting a socket with a chart-coasting Mötley anthem blasting out of the radio in the background. At that point I suspect, sparks really would start to fly!

Two early pics of Vince Neil. The insert short, which appeared in Kerrang!, was the first time that the singer had smuggled his features into any magazine anywhere.

Opposite page and below: a photo
from a session that accompanied
the band's first feature in *Sounds*
magazine, 'In five years' time
every band will look like us', they
claimed defiantly . . .

The early 'all our own work' stage set (live shot).

The US festival at San Bernadino. On May 29, 1983 (heavy metal day) the Crue followed openers Quiet Riot on a seven-band bill in front of …

... 350,000 people. According to Tommy 'we were all just freaking out'.

Opposite page: promotional shot of Tommy Lee circa the *Shout At The Devil* **LP (1983).**

Nikki and Vince from the same session.

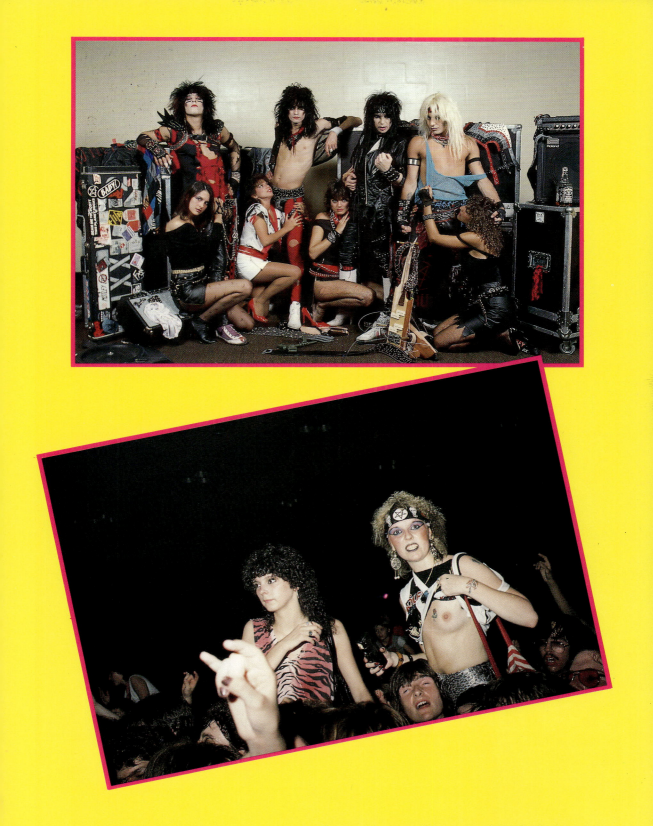

Fans and fanettes: 'We get the girls who don't waste any
time . . . we're not the type of band that's going to attract
people like Farrah Fawcett backstage to our shows.'

Motley Crue and a 'dragged-up' Ozzy
behind the scenes at the Coliseum in
Jacksonville, Florida (May 1984). Both
acts were banned from the city after
the show.

Photos taken on the set of the video 'Too Young To Fall In Love'. After two days of shooting, the forty pound mackerel was hard to be in the same city with.

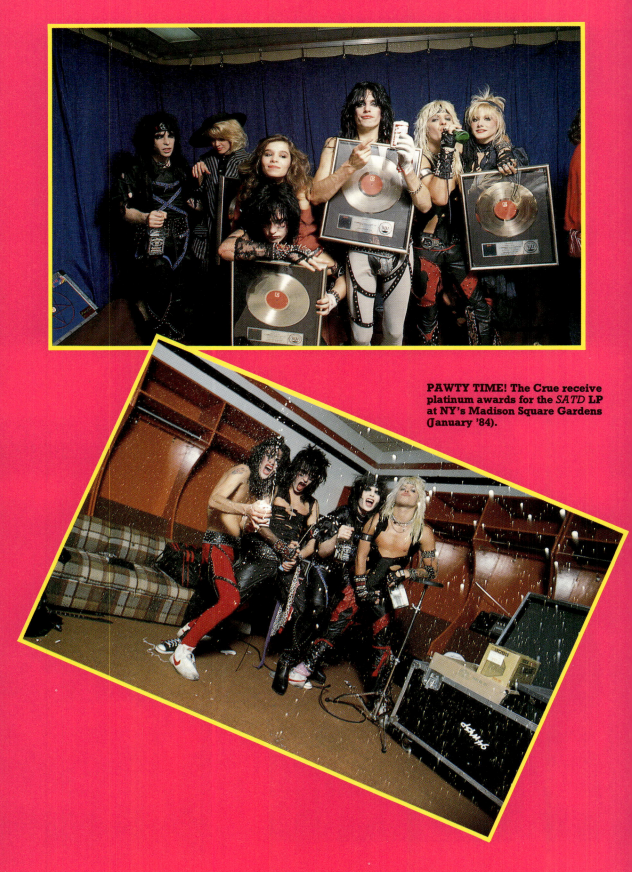

PAWTY TIME! The Crue receive platinum awards for the *SATD* **LP** at NY's Madison Square Gardens (January '84).

Tommy Lee

'I've seen too many drummers just drum and it's not very entertaining. I want to have somebody go "Hey dude, did you see that?" . . .'

IN POCKET-BOOK prose, Tommy Lee likes to do things fast and, most important, make as much noise as possible doing them. He drives fast (a powerful silver corvette), drinks fast (a powerful mouth) and talks fast (ditto), though his reading style is a little more fractured. He likes fast video games – the kind where a sudden unexpected twitch of an eyebrow can result in the entire earth being zapped by ever-advancing aliens – and give him a rayon or a felt-tip pen and he can knock you up an instant (usually obscene) doodle on the wall or arm of your choice. Indeed, it's quite possible that a certain fridge door at SIR rehearsal studios, Hollywood, still houses a few strokes from what can best be described as the climax of his 'blue period'. You get the, uh, picture?!

If not, you can always talk to his neighbours about him, they'll fill you in . . . as long as you remember to shout through a megaphone that is, 'cos being in the same vicinity (town even) as the lightning and leggy Mr Lee can easily take its toll on your hearing. It's bad enough when he gets excited, but with a stereo volume switch seemingly welded around the '10' spot, there's just no peace for the wicked or the wise. Be it blistering heavy rock or jazz, funk and fusion, anything in fact except Country & Western which Tommy has no time for whatsoever, it has to be played at teeth-gritting volume. AC/DC, Chaka Khan or the Gap Band, it all gets the same treatment. The folk next door would try banging on the wall but he'd probably only thank them for adding to the din.

'Yeah, I'm hyper, a wild man,' he says gleefully, laying bare the fringes of a prankish sense of humour, 'I play the stereo 24 hours a day!'

Tommy's impression of a bass guitar wasn't followed by Tommy's impression of a trumpet . . .

Twenty two years old and single, Tommy maintains that if he hadn't made it as a musician he'd like to have been a gynaecologist. This must come as something of a surprise to many . . . who doubtless thought he was already! SINCE THE age of three 'wildman' Tommy has been a resident of California, though his roots are to be found in Athens, Greece. His mother is Greek and his father was in Services out there, the two living for a while in Thailand before moving back to Athens where the miniature 'T-Bone' (a nickname bestowed by Mick on account of the drummer being so thin) burst onto the scene with a whoop and a holler. He hasn't shut up since . . .

As you'd expect, the Lee family still has ties in Greece and Tommy has been back to visit relatives there, but having moved across to Hacienda Heights on the US West Coast at such an early age he really doesn't remember too much of what went down in the shadow of the Parthenon. No big deal, I suspect; I mean, how much action can one kid shake at the local kindergarten, especially trapped

inside a romper suit that cancels all his best moves?!

More a Wild West Hero than a Greek God, Tommy is for all significant purposes Californian. He went to school there–that's grade school, junior high and the previously mentioned Royal Oak High School–finally linking up with a fellow seeker of mirth'n'mayhem in Vince, the pair bonded by boredom and an undying love for the low-slung guitar raunch of Aerosmith. In fact, the fourth 'Smith album, *Rocks*, ranks alongside the Hughes-Thrall release as Tommy's favourite record of all time, to be spoken of in a reverential whisper *only*. 'I've never even heard anything that comes close,' he says quietly . . .

WHEN THE four year old 'T-Bone' received his first drum-kit his joy was unconfined and his spirit magnanimous. It would have been easy for him to retire to the sanctuary of his bedroom and seal off the door, there to indulge himself in secret splendour. But no, that was altogether too selfish. Determined to share his good fortune with the world (well, the

immediate neighbours anyway), he took his best Christmas present ever out into the backyard by the pool for *all* to see and hear.

The kit itself was nothing too elaborate–an economy paper set-up with a small blinking light on the bass drum, a miniature cowbell and a cymbal constructed from some mystery alloy. Not much to speak of really, but it was a start and Tommy laid into it with a rabid zeal, the sort of lusty treatment more popularly associated with Stoneage man proposing to his mate. He hasn't looked back since . . .

The neighbours, one presumes, couldn't believe their luck; at last, a little 'music' to while away the humdrum hours and drown out all that pesky bird-song. Who needs it! And when Tommy started taking keyboard lessons *too*–his parents idea this time–they must have been hugging themselves with joy. He kept up the tuition until he was ten but: 'Eventually, it just got so hard I quit – it wasn't fun anymore. And, besides, I always *really* wanted to play drums so my heart wasn't in it. Now, though, I beat myself in the head for not sticking with it 'cos by this point I could have been incredible. I do remember a lot, however, so these days I basically just play by ear. I can sit behind a piano and come up with a real neat piece.'

As well as drums and keyboards, Tommy (just to keep the neighbours *totally* entertained) also had a third string to his bow–the accordion! A Davinchi electronic, to be precise, which he still has tucked away somewhere. He'd simply plug it into a guitar amp and distortion box and let rip with 'Smoke On The Water' encouraged to the hilt by his buddies, clearly impressed at this ingenious way of making one almighty racket. Indeed, it must often seem to adults that the primary function of parenthood is to allow junior to create as much carefree noise as possible before the onset of adolescent angst; to beat the hell out of biscuit tins and innocent tupperware and transform the harmless knitting needle into a weapon of supreme aural destruction, hammering it mercilessly against the stationary and the hollow.

Some of us, of course, grow out of this desire. We settle down, get married, tell the kids to keep their place and generally bare our chest before the pressures of a full adult existence. Others–the young at heart–never do. Tommy never did. Rather than channel his energies into something altogether more sedate, like skateboard riding on the freeway or burning down the school, he persuaded his parents to help him acquire bigger and better equipment, stuff that could transform him overnight from a precocious pop-gun into a one-man fusilade.

Now, inevitably, manufacturers are falling over themselves in the rush to drop free equipment at his feet. He has all sorts of sponsorship deals, including ones with Vic Firth (sticks), Drum Workshop (pedals), Sonor (drums) and Paiste (cymbals); the tools of the trade are his to pick'n'choose, but back in those early formative years when he *really* needed the help nothing was forthcoming and he can well remember asking his dad for five dollars to buy a new pair of sticks.

'Yeah, I was always breaking those,' he remembers, 'cos I hit real *hard*! I'd bust 'em like paper. After a while it got very expensive as I'd break cymbals all the time too and they're like 200 dollars *each*; I

'I've told you before, never phone me at my mixing desk.'

couldn't have afforded it if it wasn't for my dad giving me money and helping me out.'

Perhaps put off a little by the rampant tedium of his ivory instruction, Tommy elected not to take tuition on the drums, keeping his hand(s) in instead with the High School marching band–doing weird and wonderful things on snare drums and tri-toms–and a local drum corps. He taught them how to twirl the sticks and led his troops to glorious victory in almost every competition they entered, no doubt laying the foundation for his current drumming style – a sort of prolonged epileptic outburst with arms circling overhead whenever the beat permits.

'Man, that drum corps was *rude!*' he recalls enthusiastically, 'we had some good moves.'

The school, unfortunately, has all the trophies.

TOMMY'S PARENTS certainly supported their son financially in his quest for bigger, better and *louder* things to hit, but tucked deep down there was always the belief that when it came to the serious stuff, like making a living, y'know, he'd turn his attention towards acts of a more

conventional nature. It was therefore something of a shock, particularly to his sainted mother, when he showed up in the garage along with Tom, a Mexican friend, and a myopic guitarist called John whose glasses were so thick it was doubtful whether he could see through them at all! This, a naive blues/cover band, was Tommy's first nameless stab at the big time and his mother, not surprisingly, freaked out . . .

From that humble beginning Tommy moved on to an outfit under the banner of US101, the highlight of whose career was probably propping up the bill at a local show also featuring the moderately popular Wolfgang, two members of which have now resurfaced in the very excellent Autograph (support act to Van Halen on Roth and Co's last American tour). An outdoor concert in an Upland High School football stadium, it was Tommy's first gig under lights and quite an upmarket change from the High School dances the band usually found themselves playing. Five hundred people showed up and the '101ers went down pretty well. After a year or so the drummer grew tired of touring

Sometimes Tommy is a little shy about revealing his new stage outfits. No peeking now!

copy tunes around from one hop to the next and quit to lend both weight and wisdom to Suite 19 at the same time renouncing the scholastic cloister in favour of a painting job supplied by his uncle.

Not exactly fine art, you understand, more like condos, hotels and high rise apartments, and it certainly wasn't as glamorous or groupie-full as the rock'n'roll life, but it got him up in the world (all those high rise

apartments!) and the money was nothing to clear your nose at. Indeed, his parents thought it a highly suitable career, though Tommy himself was far from convinced, having more interest in brushes of a different sort. Steve Smith (Journey man) and Simon Phillips (session man), these were the people he had up on a pedestal, not a bunch of guys with emulsion-coated hair and paint-splattered overalls; it was always his dream to be a professional musician and when he got the chance to join Mötley Crüe he

jumped at it without doubt or delay.

'I just had a real weird feeling about this band. I never knew it would get as big as it has–all of this is still kicking me in the ass!–but I knew it would be good, so I quit working to give it all my time . . .

'Y'know, it didn't really strike me that we were a success at all until I got my first gold record. When I was given that I just started crying, I didn't know what to do. All of us just flipped out, and it was the same when I saw my picture in a magazine for the first time–I basically *freaked*!'

Mick Mars

'I guess ever since I was a kid, I've always had to be the focal point, the centre of attention, and a guitarist is kinda like the focal point in a band. I did play bass for a while but I didn't enjoy it . . .'
MICK MARS, without question, is the mystery man of Mötley Crüe. He doesn't do many interviews and seems almost determined to give as little away as possible to the press or anyone else for that matter. Suffice it to say that when he gets as far as opening his mouth it's usually to shower his tonsils rather than throw back his shoulders and soliloquise. Yeah, he enjoys a drink, he'll tell you that himself, and really there's no good reason why he shouldn't. In his time, I should imagine, he's sampled just about every tipple known to mankind and maybe shaken up a few potions of his own along the way; indeed, rumour has it that he once tried to crack a bottle of Jack Daniels over his head, clearly an experimental attempt to absorb the amber nectar through the scalp. A true trail-blazer . . .

In the privacy of his own Marina Del Rey apartment, however, he tends to plump for something a little kinder on the palate (and the head); a nice carafe of wine perhaps, dry white being his favourite, something, *anything*, to make the outside world seem a trifle more acceptable, a friendlier place. Does Mick really want to blow up the Earth? Word has it that he does and that he's organising Armageddon on his home computer, a device he likes to play around with when there isn't a woman close at hand. 'Oh, he's really twisted, psycho,' Nikki told Richard Hogan in *Circus* magazine (March '84), which may explain why he makes up his own computer games, probably involving women ('I need mucho chicks, I'm always horny and I want to marry Christie Brinkley', he

Mick—man of mystery . . .

when he was nothing more than a novice night-stalker (early Crüe features/press releases consistently claimed that Mick was from Newfoundland but this was just a way of heightening the man's mystique and for our purposes can be safely dismissed). His parents, it seems, were finding the winters back in Indiana a little tough to handle, so, with a relative–Mick's aunt–already out in the sun, they decided to up roots and join her. For the first few months, that all-important settling in period, the resident aunt did all within her power to help them out, providing an initial base from which the new arrivees were eventually able to strike out on their own; fledgling pioneers on foreign turf . . .

Mick went to school in Orange County, where his family are now based, and fared well up until the third grade at which point he 'started goofing off – I wasn't really interested. Things that I wanted to learn, I learnt, but things that I didn't want anything to do with just passed over my head.'

As well as being a factory foreman, Mick's father is also a religious minister, though in terms of the latter occupation he never once tried to draw his son away from the secular and across to his own point of passion. The guitarist has his own ideas about what goes on in that Penthouse in the stars, whether it's rented or to let, the great eternal questions, and to his credit his father never seriously attempted to alter that . . .

'Nothing was ever shoved down my throat; my father just let me do what I wanted . . .'

Which basically meant getting involved with music, and more particularly *heavy* music. As a kid he'd fooled around on toy guitars and learnt how to tune a ukelele, finally getting a 'proper' instrument from a secondhand store for about twelve dollars. He practised away and getting to grips with that also got him to grips with guitarists like Leslie West–his was the sort of stuff he listened to–though at school none of the other musicians wanted to play with him . . .

'They just thought I was a chump,' confesses Mick, 'though now they're still playing in their little 'Top 40' bands and I'm voted part of the number one act in America (MC topped *Hit Parader*

assures), and has perhaps the most infuriating telephone answer machine in the western hemisphere . . .

Dring! Dring!
'Hello'
'Hi, Mick, this is ..'
'Hey, can you speak up a bit?'
'OK, HI MICK, THIS . . .'
'No, you'll have to speak up'
'ALRIGHT, HI MICK . . .!!!'
'It's no good, I can't hear you, and the reason I can't hear you is because I'm not here at the moment and you're speaking to my answer machine . . .'

I'm surprised anyone bothers to phone back . . .

With bloodshot, ever-shaded eyes and six-feet-under skin tone, Mick isn't the healthiest looking soul ever to spank the plank. Descriptions of him range from a 'dazed ferret' through to 'Jiminy Cricket', the latter pearl of wisdom dropping directly from the lips of Ozzy Osbourne who we shall come

to later, oh yes. And *my* contribution? Well, a while back I described Mötley Crüe as championing the double-Jack-Daniels-and-coke-live-fast-die-young-have-a-good-looking-corpse mentality, going on to suggest that the twenty nine year old Mick could justifiably claim to have one already, the result perhaps of his vast preference for night-time over day. Put him in a sun-kissed room and the first thing he's likely to do is knot together the curtains and paint the walls black. I mean, Dracula had more am flexibility than this guy . . .

'Yeah, I like the dark far better than the light,' he concedes, 'though I don't mind a few hours of daylight . . . now and then. The only trouble is sunlight ages you faster!'

LIKE NIKKI and Tommy, Mick isn't originally from Los Angeles, having moved out to the West Coast from Terre Haute, Indiana, magazine's 1984 Readers' Poll with 137,464 votes, beating Van Halen into second place), who has the last laugh, y'know?!'

AT SEVENTEEN Mick quit school and became, by his own definition, a 'bum'. You've heard of the good old days, right? Well, these were the other thing, and there's no question that the man is a good deal happier now, enjoying the respect of friends and knowing that he doesn't have to notch-in his belt.

'I guess I didn't really do anything that paid until I was nineteen,' he recalls. 'I would just go out and buy bags of these little mini-whites (speed), eat those all the time and hitch-hike around at night with my guitar over my shoulder. I remember going up to Fresno once–I was in an all-black band (well, *almost*!)–and to make some extra money I got a job picking water melons. That's the truth!'

In between mouthfuls of mini-whites, Mick did some work with motorcycles, got a job as a security guard and eventually ended up in an industrial laundromat dealing with big 600 pound tubs, though when he gashed his hand on the machinery he knew it was time to give in his cards while he still had fingers left to do so. At that time he was part of a lightweight cover band playing out in Riverside; he'd see to the dirty laundry by day (good training for Mötley Crüe!), then play his guitar 'till maybe six in the morning and still hit the dawn air with barely enough cash to live on.

'God,' he smiles woefully, shaking his head, 'those were the most depressing days of my life. I never *ever* want to do that again!'

He's serious. *Very*. Not wanting to slip back into that sort of existence–hand to mouth with no food in the hand–is what keeps him permanently aware and never too comfortable with current status or success. Like the shootists of the Old West, the established guns, the ones with the most notches on their fretboards can never rest easy, never put their feet up on the tethering rail, knowing that there's a whole gaggle of little (hoping to be) big men just itching to catch them with their trigger finger relaxed and the sun in their eyes. Mick knows the score . . .

"There's just so many good guitar players running around now, young kids, and it scares me to death. So I'm gonna have to keep my own style but improve it–

without doing what they're doing, the hammer-ons and all that kind of stuff. I can do those things but I don't want to because everybody else does.'

On the whole, Mick likes to keep things pretty simple, reckoning taste more important than speed. If the song demands a fast solo, a sudden cascade of the fingers, then he's well able to take two paces forward, strike a stance and *burn* (tune into 'Use It Or Lose It' on the *Theatre of Pain* LP for ample evidence of this). Usually he prefers to play with the senses rather than the stopwatch, delivering from a level somewhere between the gut and the crotch

with no overblown ego to get in the way. He doesn't move as much on-stage as Nikki and Vince, it's true, but before he linked up with Mötley Crüe he was 'more like a Tony Iommi' so just count yourselves lucky, right?!'

It sounds a mite pompous, I know, but I guess you could call Mick a 'people's player'; someone (self-taught) who doesn't give a flying pick for technical dos and don'ts as long as it sounds good; someone who doesn't have a huge guitar collection gathering dust at home, preferring to work his instruments out on the road (with the single exception of a late '50's Silvertone); someone who'd rather

put in a performance the fans can understand and relate to than baffle them with a senseless scramble of digits and the usual pained visage. He feels he's suffered plenty for his art already . . .

PRE-MÖTLEY CRÜE Mick drifted around from one local band to the next–some original, mostly copy–without really getting anywhere . . .

'I was going "I'm starving to death, I'd better do something", and I wasn't about to get a *real* job, so I just played in these stupid 'Top 40' combos for a few months to get myself together then went back to the original stuff again.'

In all his other enterprises the guitarist has had to adapt personal technique–a succession of 'pig squeals' evenly dispersed over a solid hard riff base–to suit the background presence of either a keyboardist or a rhythm man, but having established a solo niche for himself within the Crüe and clearly relishing the extra space, he feels that any addition now would only cramp his style. And the other enterprises? Well, let's see . . . There was White Horse, Vendetta, who he encouraged to play original material against a tidal wave of apathy, and Video Nu-r, with whom he did 'a few little dumb records. They were kinda punk meets new wave, but I was more like a guest on the stuff they did. I'd worked with the guys before but they broke up then reformed and didn't ask me to play, though when they entered the studio they did want me to help out so I went for it . . .'

And now he's going for it on a full-time, hell-for-leather basis with the Crüe, enjoying a few of the trappings of success (like a car!), though the upward road has certainly been littered with its fair share of boulders and the occasional oily turn. Not easy–by no means. Behind the black glass stare and the even blacker fringe lurks an honorary graduate of the school of hard knocks, someone who's been there and back then back for more, yet never once considered tossing in the towel. God, there were times when he was lucky to *own* a towel . . .

'Ex-wives would bitch at me and friends would too; they'd go out to their jobs and drive up in a new car, and I was like a bum with no car, but I refused to give in. Now when I got back to see some of my friends they say "man, I wish *I'd* stuck with it . . ." ' I'm sure they do.

Act Four Local Heroes

'One of the few groups that has actually turned The Troubadour audience into a minor riot. Amazing music – every song is catchy. I think there is no stopping Mötley Crüe' – Bobby Dean, booking agent, The Troubadour, 1981

BY THE Summer of '81 Nikki and his hand-picked pirate team were ready to make some serious local moves. The band finally had the frontman they wanted, a thousand records with which to grease hungry palms and an enthusiastic manager who'd lovingly embraced the Crüe Cause. In fact, the boyz hadn't really wanted a manager in the fullest sense of the term, more a financial backer, someone to sign his name at the bottom of their dreams, but Allan Coffman clearly didn't appreciate the 'benign patron' role envisaged for him. At an initial meeting he gave the group some fifty dollars for food and essential supplies – which they used to buy a gram of coke – and from that point on he had at least one digit in every doughnut.

In terms of experience, Coffman – falsely hailed as a millionaire by *Music Express* magazine (issue 59) – had little to offer being the owner of a construction company in Grass Valley as well as a member of the zoning administration; however, he *was* on the lookout for a likely project to invest in and Mötley Crüe certainly needed the support. Allan's brother-in-law, the curiously labelled Stick, simply mentioned a close guitarist friend of his called Mick Mars and the band he was playing with, and in the blink of an eye and the clink of a glass Coffman & Coffman Productions (so dubbed to credit wife Barbara) was a viable music biz force poised to put Brian Epstein and the like to darkened, hollow shame. Today California, tomorrow . . . *Northern* California. Yes, that's right, a tour (June 10-30), taking in Chico, Fresno, the Bay Area, Nevada city (The Nevada Theatre, June 18) and Grass Valley (the marvellously named Tommyknacker, 19/20) . . .

'Grass Valley is one of those towns where it just says "Main Street" and that's the only street there is,' says Vince. 'We show up there and go into this bar and Nikki's got on these yellow pants and this big red belt, our hair's all spiked up and we're wearing stiletto boots, *everything*, y'know, and the place is just full of bikers and hippies. We really didn't fit in at all!'

'Actually, the first time we did a radio interview was up there, but it wasn't for a rock station, more like an adult contemporary one. So the interviewer asks "how did the band form?" and everyone immediately points at Nikki who goes "ah . . . ah . . . ah . . .". In the end, Allan had to tell the story; they put a microphone in front of us and we just clammed up, we didn't know *what* to do!'

Grass Valley certainly wasn't a Mötley Mecca, though (as already detailed) the four did play a couple of their early gigs there, including a never-to-be-forgotten appearance in the *'yeehaw!'* environs of a cowboy bar . . .

'There was no stage,' recalls Vince, 'just chicken wire around us, and I guess it had been promoted as a Hollywood dress-up night or something. It was really ridiculous 'cos these cowboys had no idea how to dress; this one guy came chained to two girls and they were dancing around like that! Meantime, we were playing our songs but they weren't going over too well; there was hardly a soul in the place anyway, just a bunch of old guys sitting at the bar plus, of course, this other guy and these chicks still chained together dancing! We kept saying "let's do 'Johnny B. Goode' again" – we did that about five times and 'Train Kept A Rollin'' four times . . .'

Not all shows, however, proved such a dead horse; back home in LA, on more fertile turf, the tearaway High School crowds required very

Motley Crue breaks out in Nevada County stint

By JIM BURNS
Staff Writer

They stand out in rural, slow-moving Nevada County.

But the Northern California pace has not affected the stinging music that happens when this Hollywood quartet get together for some fiery rock'n roll.

Tuesday, they jammed at Lyman Gilmore School auditorium. Motley Crue, as the group is called, was getting ready for its Nevada County — and Northern California — debut, which will occur Thursday at 8 p.m. in the Nevada Theater in Nevada City.

There will be no drinks served which gives one an idea what kind of crowd this long-haired, punk-looking band is catering to.

Most of their audiences — at least in the L.A. area — have started at age 13 and gone up from there. The band, says Nikki Sixx, the group's 22-year-old bass guitarist, songwriter and spokesman, plays music the younger set can relate to.

For instance, the group's "Public Enemy" is a song Sixx thinks most teenagers can bite their teeth into.

Sixx and other band members — Mick Mars, 25, lead guitar; Tommy Lee, 21, drums; Vince Neal, 21, lead vocals — think they're on the brink of stardom.

Together just three months, the group has already received great reviews for performances at the Whisky a Go Go and Starwood. "We're definitely a success in LA already," Sixx says with no hesitation.

"It's been magic from day one," chimes in drummer Lee.

wny suddenly a show in Grass Valley?

This is where Coffman & Coffman Productions has been established to manage the band. Allan Coffman, general contractor and member of the county board of zoning administration, and wife Barbara, Grass Valley School District board member, discovered the band through Barbara's brother.

The Coffmans flew to Los Angeles for a look at the group. They liked what they saw. Now, they are the group's financial backers.

"This is at the forefront of a rebirth of rock 'n roll," Allan says, dismissing the group's punk-like looks.

"It's because they look different that people think they must be punk," Barbara adds.

No way is the group punk-oriented, Sixx says. "That's destruction. They (punkers) like to smash their heads into walls, slash their wrists. We're just different. Maybe a little ahead of our times. Maybe in five years, every band will look like us."

Besides, adds singer Neal, punk musicians "don't like us. Our hair is too long."

Their music is definitely hard-driving rock. And just to make sure the audience knows that, "they've put a couple of Elvis and Beatles numbers in their repertoire," Barbara says.

The Coffmans think the band will take off when it gets a recording contract. "We'll break **through** when we get our first recording," Sixx says.

The group will follow up its Nevada Theater date with Friday and Saturday shows at the Tommyknacker. From there it's on to the Bay Area and Chico for scheduled dates.

little flogging indeed. They were going Crüe crazy, simple as that, locking hearts and souls at the vanguard of a genuine *movement*, and once Vince gave up his job wiring restaurants to concentrate on wiring a real live crowd, *les bon Möts* were able to head for broke without dip or deviation, pumping all available money into what was fast becoming a dream come true. They had a clear sight of where they were heading, even if Tommy couldn't quite make up his mind what to put on his bass drums (a heartbeat signal, an air-raid motif . . .), and nothing or no-one was going to catch their heels on the way. Determination they had; a little money to go with it would have been nice . . .

'For a while after I quit my job I was living in the back of Tommy's van in his driveway,' says Vince. 'I was there for about a month and then his parents took pity on me so I started staying with them. Then we all moved into this apartment near The Whisky A Go Go that Allan had set up for us – except for Mick, that is, who was living with a bunch of people in Redondo Beach and being driven to and from rehearsals by Stick. We would play and pay the rent with that money and the rest would go into clothes and stuff like that. Allan had us on a budget of twenty dollars a week each!'

'The way we'd survive was by going out and picking up on chicks, having them get us food, or saying "hey, can I come over and eat dinner tonight?" I mean, you can spend twenty dollars in a bar in one night, so Nikki and myself would walk across the street to the liquor store, buy real cheap vodka and go drink it with the bums before heading off to the clubs. That way we wouldn't have to buy drinks when we got there, we could save money, but it was very tough . . .'

'We stole turkey pies at Thanksgiving and trees at Christmas, things like that, because we couldn't get them any other way. We didn't have *anything* and we were always in jail for one reason or another, we just seemed to attract trouble. We couldn't even shut the front door of our apartment properly because the police had kicked it in so many times! It was *that* bad . . .'

It was indeed. In a grossout interview in *Oui* magazine (November '82) Vince revealed not only that a prime band pastime was giving 'tongue baths' to eleven year old girls, but also that whilst in the old dwelling they hadn't always been able to afford toilet paper

being forced back quite often on either Nikki's old socks or a map of New York. Ah well, I guess Central Park wasn't too green *that* year . . . TUCKED AWAY in his current apartment, Vince has a scrapbook containing a host of old photos and clippings, a complete blow-by-blow record of the band's early history. These days he doesn't particularly bother with all that – there's simply too much written about the group to make it possible and seeing his name in print probably isn't the buzz that it once was – but to begin with at least there was little that escaped his attention and that of his Instamatic. Indeed, should said file ever fall into unscrupulous hands, certain parties not entirely unconnected with the Crüe corner might well choose to crawl into brown paper bags or bury themselves in the garden.

It's all there in black and white and often full colour; the unfashionable (a Polaroid of Mick in cherished blue leggings), the unexpected (Allan Coffman handing over dollar bills to a visibly shaken Tommy – a genuinely rare, perhaps unique, shot) and the unfed (a photo of Nikki fresh out of the shower with hair lathered into a 'mohawk' and ribs on the outside – virtually!). Were this particular snap ever to make it onto peak-time TV news there can be no question that rock legends the world over would instantly join hands and hearts to sing for *his* supper, and it's just amazing that the bassist's name wasn't instantly altered to Nikki Stixx. a missed opportunity . . .

'Well, the thing is, we never used to eat,' explains Vince laughing, which might just account for it.

Clearly, what the band needed was a wealthy record company to spirit them away from the manner to which they'd become accustomed. They had the fire in their bellies, all they needed now was the food to go with it. To this end, they embarked on the traditional course of touting a demo tape around the companies but, according to Nikki, 'they all said we were too weird. Everything was wrong; either our songs were too heavy metal or they were too pop, so we just thought, well, we have a large following who we believe want the music, let's go ahead and give it to 'em!'

This they duly did, the Crüe's debut *Too Fast For Love* album being, in effect, a spruced-up demo recorded and mixed at Hit City West studio inside a week. The band elected to produce themselves and managed to keep costs down to around 8,000 dollars – money

advanced by Coffman, though he was later paid back with the proceeds from live shows.

'A really dirty sounding record', is Nikki's joyful description of the finished product – issued in December '81 complete with lyric sheet – though in order to achieve the desired level of grime'n'grind it was first of all necessary to dispose of a particularly irksome engineer. More used to dealing with techno-pop than heavy rock bands he just couldn't get a grip on the Crüe way of doing things so Michael Wagener, who's since gone on to work with the likes of Great White, Malice and LA punk/metal mutants X, was brought

in to fix things up, doing a suitably seedy job.

As for the packaging of the album, well that was down to the band alone. On the front of the sleeve they chose to display Vince's heavily adorned lower abdomen (the interesting bit with one of the vocalist's hands forming a sign that some might take to mean the 'devil's horns' but the deaf will acknowledge as the symbol for 'I Love You'), along with the title of the record and the Sixx-sculptured logo that had already graced the cover of the single, while on the back they placed the results of a photo session with a certain Michael Pinter. A

friend of Coffman's, he had been heavily briefed and flown in from San Francisco especially for the assignment . . .

'The trouble is, though,' explains Vince, 'he took the pictures from up on a ladder so our legs are really short! He shot us *down* and it makes us look stupid. I think the guy was just a baby photographer or something like that; he'd never done anything like this before.'

'Also, Nikki and myself tried to tell him that he couldn't photograph us against a white background because my hair wouldn't show up. He said "don't worry about it!" so what happened was you couldn't see

my hair *at all* and it had to be touched up.'

Touched up it was indeed, though seriously molested might be a more accurate description; an embarrassingly extravagant salvage job that turned an innocent Rod Stewart tease into a real 'Bonanza' special (so called due to the sudden explosive resemblance between the singer's crowning glory and a luxuriant ball of tumble-weed).

When Vince saw the results he simply couldn't believe his eyes, but by that time it was too late to change anything – for the moment, at least. Hence, the first two thousand copies of the record had the reluctant Mr Neil with head encased in a candy-floss cocoon (he doesn't own one of those!), but for the next pressing this air-brushed aureole was significantly reduced, and while they were tampering around the band also decided to add a touch of colour to the black and white cover by pricking logo and title and letting them bleed (they tinted them red). The LP *did* remain on the Crüe's own label, but by this point they'd had to change the spelling from Leäther to *Leathür*, their original choice being already spoken for.

Altogether, around 30,000 copies of these initial pressings were eventually sold, though at first the band simply made them available at gigs and walked them round to local record stores, and it wasn't until the Greenworld distribution company got involved that Vince's below-the-belt blow-up really started to travel. Discerning kids in San Francisco and San Diego could now get hold of the record and a few copies even filtered across to Europe where the response of the press was both sudden and supportive. In the States, *Billboard* magazine was *almost* converted, saying that 'with Cheap Trick (at least temporarily) in eclipse, this is just the sort of band that could fill the gap', but it was the British papers which really went to town, frothing and foaming with unnatural abandon. Mop-tops, music, the seedy rag-doll chic, it was all OK in the UK . . .

In *Kerrang!* (issue 10 February 25-March 10 1982), for example, Sammy Gee described the 'TFFL' album as 'chock-full of hedonistic charm' and 'a tight-trousered, back-combed delight', going on to highlight the troupe's 'Roth-approved allure', while the full page/full colour pic of Vince on page twenty one of the same issue was the first time he'd got his face (and other assorted bits) into *any*

magazine *anywhere*.

'Someone showed it to me while I was sitting in the bar at The Troubadour,' he recalls, 'and I *flipped!*'

In the absence of any more reliable information, the caption accompanying the pic of Vince was dragged, still gushing, from the band's first biog. It claimed that Mötley Crüe represented a return to 'the hard driving sound of the Beatles re-energised for the '80's' and that Vince's 'unique styling and versatile range is influenced by John Lennon and Robin Zander (of Cheap Trick) . . .'

In fact, Vince is far from the world's greatest Beatles' fan and his on-stage manner derives more from Steven Tyler's raggedy mikestand and raggedy ass allure than Robin Zander's entire pretty boy being. But it all sounded good and gave the press something to sink their teeth into. Geoff Barton, in particular, showed no inclination to languish on the fence, leaping o'er it instead in full-pelt praise of a band who seemed to represent an unabashed return to the heyday of 'glitter rock', precursors perhaps of a 'brand new shock rock wave'.

Reviewing the *TFFL* LP in *Sounds* (January 23 1982), he alliterated wildly and raved unrestrained, dropping a whole host of prime reference points (Sweet, Cheap Trick, Angel, Eddie Van Halen, Starz, The Glitter Band, Randy Rhoads, Girl, UFO) and summing up the plastic as 'one of the most spectacular debuts you're ever likely to hear'. An illicit confection of gutter-level goodies, he rated every song bar none and the readers weren't inclined to disagree, pushing 'Piece Of Your Action' (track five, side one) to 'Number One' in *Sounds*'American Albums/Heavy Metal' chart and 'Live Wire' (track one, side one) to number eight.

Clearly, there was nothing polished or refined about this mob or their music – put the record on the turntable and you had to fight to keep the flies away! – but the appeal of both was undeniable; a kind of juvenile, beneath-the-sheets appeal similar to the thrill of kicking a tin can over early morning cobbles or ringing the doorbell of a sore-headed neighbour then heading for the nearest privet. Mötley Crüe were, and still are, big kids in tight trousers, too cöol for Sköol, and when word came that they might be crossing the Atlantic for a series of shows (their first outside the States) the middle digit of every Euro sleazeball suddenly underwent an

involuntary erection. The band, metal/pop anthems nicely primed, were on the watery march east; nothing could stop them now . . . could it?

HEAVY ROCK fans in the UK were pounding the pavements with excitement and parents, brows furrowed and nerves in tatters, were sealing off the bedrooms of their female offspring as fast as shaking hands would allow. Chicken-wire and heavy chain, goose-fat and garlic, all were used with a cunning vision 'cos on an occasion such as this it was best not to trust to chance. Was it just a trick of the light or had the sky suddenly darkened? And where had that wind come from, sharp and marrow-cold? In living rooms across the land cats crouched tensely in their baskets, hackles on alert, while out in the forest, shawl drawn taut across wizened frame, the old gypsy women crossed herself slowly in silent prayer. The writing was on the wall – not to mention *Sounds* and *Kerrang!*; Wishbone Ash had apparently lined up a European tour for late March/early April '82 and Mötley Crüe were all set to support, with the possibility of extra dates of their own in the UK.

The word was out, the hair-spray holocaust poised to begin, though somebody had clearly forgotten to tell Wishbone Ash who just a few weeks later were denying all knowledge of Mötley Crüe in print. A spokesperson for the English outfit told *Sounds* (April 24) that 'I've never seen or heard of this band' and that the Ash had no European tour planned anyway, being currently in the studio working on an album. All very strange . . .

'Allan Coffman told us that Wishbone Ash were frightened to have us open for them on the tour,' says a still baffled Vince, 'but I don't think anybody *really* knows what happened. I did see a telex with all the dates on it, though, so there must have been *some* truth in the whole thing.'

In terms of European acceptance, the Wishbone Ash 'are they?/aren't they?' scenario did Mötley Crüe no good at all. Fans of the band, whipped up by heavy press coverage, unusual for an act both unsigned and distant, were clearly disappointed and there was worse to come; in particular a rumour (which also made it into print – *Sounds* April 24/May 8) that the four would be embarking on a hammer-

Crüesing for love

MÖTLEY CRÜE
'Too Fast For Love'
(Leathür Records
LR-123)*****

"IT'S KIND of like back to the early days of, I hate to say 'glitter', but during that era everything was real exciting. From there, music just seemed to regress..."

Never was a truer word said! Forget the passing of the Pistols/Clash/Jam jubilee, ignore the demises of any number of so-called rock revolutions — when the Double-G hung up his platforms, when the Sweet abandoned their Indian headdresses, when Flintlock first found their gunpowder damp, that was the day the music died. And since then it's been strictly doooown-hill.

The man behind the quote at the beginning of this review is unlikely-named unfashionable thinker Nikki Sixx. And, of course, he's referring to the sleazoid style of the band he plays the bass with: the umlaut-laden Mötley Crüe.

The Crüe are heading the crest of a brand new shock rock wave — what a way to start the New Year! Formed in Los Angeles last February, this tinsel team proclaim that they are 'the commercial hard rock band the '80s have been screaming for'.

I wouldn't argue with that and neither, it seems, would the Southern California concert-going public. Within six months of coming together les bon Möts set an all-time attendance record at the Hollywood Troubadour and sold out the Country Club and the Whiskey A-Go-Go. They also became one of a handful of acts to play the Roxy Theater without the benefit of record company support.

With music big non-veteran manager Allan Coffman supplying the readies, MC recorded a demo tape, from which a single 'Stick To Your Guns'/'Toast Of The Town' was taken. It was warmly received and this here album follows quickly, (a limited edition [pending national distribution deal] on the band's own Leathür Records label.

And wouldja believe it's one of the most spectacular debuts you're ever likely to hear? Yeah, Mr Sixx, vocalist Vince Neil, guitarist Mick Mars and drummer Tommy Lee have produced a real lip poutin' powerhouse of a pose-platter.

With influences like the Sweet and Cheap Trick and image similarities to Angel, it'll come as no surprise to you to hear that Mötley Crüe hardly attract a 'mature' American audience; rather 'they start at age 13 and go up from there'.

But the immediacy of Mötley music is such that I'm sure that even the grubbiest, greasiest, most prejudiced UK HM fan will see beyond the ludicrous looks and start grinding his studded wristbands with glee.

Just one listen to album opener 'Live Wire' and you won't be so much hooked as' bloodily impaled: a guitar riff of Suterian brutality, a coupla Eddie Van Halen-style octave-pings and suddenly you're riding the rails with a trash-metal teen teaser par excellence. Neil squeals the words 'Cos I'm ALIVE! Live WHY-AllIIR!' like Robin Zander with his foot in a bear trap and the band display the brash confidence of a gang of street-strutting Puerto Ricans: a bunch who may look puny but who know they're tough.

Side one continues with 'Public Enemy Number One', a glorious Starz-reminiscent Glamthem, complete with tongue-in-rouged-cheek 'Oh yeah's and 'Hey-hey-hey's and G-Band stomp-chorus.

'Take Me To The Top' marks a return to murder-style metal, vocalist Vince ascending to skyriser heights and then revealing a lemming-like deathwish with the words '...And throw me off!'

The jeans-creaming 'Merry-Go-Round' provides a balladic breather and then you're off with the LP's tour de force, 'Piece Of Your Action'

This staggering standout has everything, from the taunting screams of 'Yeow!' and 'Ooh yea-ah!' at the start to the stunningly inventive guitar solo at the finish. Mick Mars staking a claim to become the hottest new axe hero since Randy Rhoads. And of course the lyrics leave little to the imagination: Tight action, rear traction / So hot you really blow me away / Fast moving, wet and ready / The time is right so hold on tight!'

Although side two has nothing to touch 'Action', I'd hate for you to pass it over completely. 'Starry Eyes', 'Come On And Dance' and 'Too Fast For Love' maintain a high standard of 'Rock And Roll Over'-style heavy pop perfection. 'Dance' is particularly memorable for the delightful line 'In a Pepsi sheen, she's a leather tease' and 'Too Fast' is a breathless story of a Californian hussy with insatiable sexual desires.

'Stick To Your Guns' is the odd track out, a jerking anomaly kinda like Girl's 'My Number', and LP closer 'On With The Show' is a graphic UFO-type tale of the comeuppance of a show-off switchblade slashing punk.

Have-I succeeded in whetting your appetite? If not, you better believe that, far from being glitter rock's last gasp, Mötley Crüe are more like its second coming! Or, in the immortal words of Kick-Ass Kevin Kozak: 'Shock rock, rock 'n' roll, we're gonna give it to you — RED HOT!'

< The above review of **TOO FAST FOR LOVE** appeared in the 23 January edition of SOUNDS magazine [U.K.]. >

and-thongs co-headlining tour of the UK with Canadian rockers Anvil, the pair of them stopping off at the Reading Festival over August Bank Holiday before heading off together around the country. None of it, of course, finally came to pass, and to make matters worse it all had that vapid, though bitter, taste traditionally associated with arch West Coast hype.

All across Britain hairdos deflated overnight.

BACK IN Los Angeles, looking in on all these denials and counter denials, the band themselves were having something of a frustrating time. Being ultra-determined not to chase their tails around the local club circuit, they were patently peeved that plans to go forth (and multiply) on a European tour hadn't come together as they should, and then there was the little matter of an assault charge against Nikki. He was leaving the Rainbow with Vince and a couple of girls one night when, according to the singer, 'these bikers started to hassle us. So we got into a fight and, all of a sudden, the cops pulled up. Nikki had this guy down on the ground and was swinging a chain that he'd taken from around his waist, but when one of the cops came over he caught him with it right on the head . . . I didn't go to jail that night, though Nikki did, and by the time I picked him up the cops had nailed him good.'

'I only had to wear eye make-up on one eye for a few gigs,' the beaten bassist told Chris Morris in Reader magazine (November 25, 1983), 'the other eye was definitely black.'

And in Kerrang! (issue 57, December 15-28 1983) . . .

'They wanted to send me to state prison for five years with no probation or parole – assaulting a police officer with a deadly weapon. But the system here is so corrupt that the girl I was going out with at the time hocked her car, got 1000 dollars and gave the money to the cops. After that, the charges were dropped.'

Much to the relief of local rock fans, no doubt, for by this point Mötley Crüe were up'n'coming at an almost frightening pace, being hailed by Stu Simone in BAM magazine (April 9 1982) as the 'fastest rising band Los Angeles has seen in ages'. Those debut shows at The Starwood enabled them to win over Y&T's crowd and after that they had little trouble winning over their own: Oz Records and Tarzana sold sixty copies of the Too Fast For Love album within four days of its release and Licorice Pizza, a record, tapes and video store opposite The Whisky, got rid of all its stock straight away, no problem. The smart money was betting that the four Crüesters would reach stardom in five years . . . and go deaf in six!

Already they'd triumphed in the local clubs: The Troubadour (September 1981), The Roxy (November 12 1981, headlining over Dokken) and The Whisky A Go Go, playing there on December 11/12 1981, January 15 1982 above Stormer and three Valentine's Day weekend shows in conjunction with *BAM* magazine on February 12/13/14. DuBrow opened up for two of the nights and A La Carte the third, and all three were sell-outs with fans lining up right around the block to ensure a ticket and a decent view, a scene paralleling the rise to glory of a former Southern California club band called Van Halen. You must have heard of 'em . . .

In between, there were shows at The Country Club (Christmas Day 1981) and Oxnard Auditorium (the day after) and a return visit to The Troubadour for a New Year's Eve extravaganza with Stormer and American Heroes also on the bill. Yet it was a SRO gig at The Country Club on Saturday March 13 1982 with A La Carte and Wolfgang in tow that really underlined the band's ever-swelling status. Stu Simone was in the audience, notebook poised and lead wetted, witnessing three no-holds-barred encores and 'nothing but post-show smiles on the faces of

the drained fans leaving the club'. He was much impressed, speaking of 'unstoppable momentum', 'flashy attire', a 'glitzy stage set-up' and a 'well choreographed light show', lost in the all-angles entertainment of a group committed to the music certainly, yet committed to a great deal more besides. Back in September '81 Bruce Duff had commented in *Music Connection* (Vol. V No. 19) that Tommy's 'stick-twirling gimmickry coupled with an unusual method of switch-hitting his various blows and crashes make for a show in itself', which was pretty much the idea . . .

'The way we come on is not like we're here to shock people', Nikki told Rob Jones from Cerritos High School (October 15 1982) 'we come on like this is entertainment-we're going to give you a full show, visually and musically, with all the props and everything else we can bring. Anything for entertainment. We don't get paid extra for doing that, so obviously we love it'.

In *Music Connection* (Vol. VI No. 4 February 18-March 3 1982) Mick let his imagination run a little wilder . . .

'The ultimate would be to put on something like a full-scale Broadway production', he told Michael Heller, 'but on a more modern rock oriented level. The flash just adds to the excitement'.

With that pronouncement glowing neon bright inside the collective Crüe consciousness, the band lined up a show at the 3,500 capacity Santa Monica Civic in April 1982, an opportunity for them to indulge OTT instincts to the maximum, and air an angry new number 'Knock 'Em Dead, Kid', inspired it seems by those fair-minded pillars of truth, justice, etc. the LAPD. The concert, put on by a racing car promoter (Steve Quercio & Race Track Promotions), was yet another success, the four sharing the big stage with a couple of dragster cars and setting fire to various instruments – sensibly at the end of proceedings – yet still Mötley Crüe remained peripheral, their onset resisted by those at the hub of the LA music scene.

Their popularity, and the *fervour* of that popularity, was beyond dispute – they could prove that any night in any club and beleaguered radio station switchboards would return the self-same tale – yet they remained without a recording deal or significant radio support. Sure, Joe Benson's *Local Music Show* on KL05 was aware of their existence, but with corporate American radio essentially controlled by consultants interested in an older demography and hence more polished rock bands, it was hard for these (very) rough diamonds to get a heel in the door.

'We'd invite record company people down to see us all the time,' says Vince, 'but nobody wanted to know.'

Allan Coffman being an industry outsider didn't help matters, of course, but that was only part of the story; without wishing to sound melodramatic or maudlin, I think it's fair to say that the Crüe were misunderstood. *Very.* Mick has a favourite saying, but I couldn't possibly reproduce it in these pages so I'll tell you one I can. Here goes: 'the first thing people do when they see a spider is kill it – they don't try to understand it', which for my money has a definite ring of truth. To certain people in certain quarters, Mötley Crüe were an unknown quantity, ingredient X, scuttling along the skirting board or poised by the plug-hole, and the immediate reaction was either to lash out hard with a size twelve Nike or else head off screaming in the opposite direction.

'Yeah, people were really intimidated by us,' explains Vince, "cos when we entered a club we were always dressed to the hilt – black leather, gloves, make-up, y'know – and we'd all walk in together like gunslingers from the Old West. No-one was sure how to talk to us, and if they *did* talk to us whether we would turn round and smack 'em!'

And jealousy? Did that exist too?

'Yeah, because a lot of the other bands had been playing the circuit for a good many years – Mr DuBrow, for instance, he'd been around for ten years or something like that and then we come along and he's got to open for us. I guess at one point it really went to our heads; we changed a little, but then we levelled off. I'm sure people thought we were the biggest assholes who ever walked the earth!'

That's as maybe, but one thing the Crüe could never be accused of lacking was confidence in themselves. If someone stared in horror, they barely noticed, and still don't ('when I walk into most any place people stare, but I never pay attention to that, it doesn't bother me' – Nikki), and if someone called them cocky they'd probably agree, complementing their accusor on his (or her) powers of perception. Some rock stars have bodyguards, Nikki and co have an attitude which is theirs and theirs alone. It surrounds

Review of The Country Club show on March 13, 1982, a SRO gig underlining the band's ever-swelling status.

and protects them, unites them when necessary and pervades all they do in terms of music and style. There's no cracks or concessions, no quarter . . .

'The thing is,' says Vince, 'you've gotta convince people that yours is the cool way to look and that they look like idiots. Once they start thinking that then you've got 'em!' BACK IN the days when Vince was surreptitiously smoking Angel Dust in the maths class at school (why no need to retreat to the boy's room?) 'Well, I had this pipe that looked like a pen and no smoke ever came out!'), Mick and Nikki were constantly changing their image, adjusting the vision that greeted them in the mirror. The former, fed up looking like a 'real pale surfer', was shifting through the spectrum from blond to blue-black, while the latter was experimenting wildly with red and white – both separately and combined – eventually opting for an inky top himself, dangerously spiked of course. Inexorably, through trial and error, the pair (indeed, the four) found themselves treading common ground, hitting naturally on cuts and costumes that today represent an integral element of rock'n'roll culture, making their mark on fans and musicians alike.

Roll up! Roll up! get your 'Crüe Gloves' mail order through the US music press, and down on Hollywood and Vine there's an entire store designed to keep hard-core Mötley minions in sartorial touch with their heroes; it's even got a painting of Vince outside just to make the point absolutely clear! A sure sign of success, yet not *that* long ago Mötley Crüe, mavericks all, couldn't get themselves arrested in LA . . . No, that's not right; they *could* get themselves arrested but acceptance from the business side was a little harder to come by. Not surprising, therefore, that when a contract was finally slapped down on the desk it didn't derive from any local source. They'd all passed, leaving a London (England) based record company to take two paces forward dipped quill in hand. It was swiftly arranged. The next morning Mötley Crüe would sign with Virgin Records.

LIVE ACTION

Motley Crue
The Country Club
March 13

APRIL 9, 1982/BAM

After easily selling out the prestigious Country Club, Motley Crue devastated the SRO crowd Saturday night with a blistering set that served as a farewell hometown performance before they embark on a tour of Europe which will cover eleven countries. In the space of a year, glitter / metal / pop-rockers Motley Crue have metamorphosed from two young musicians trying to get something together in a Hollywood apartment to the fastest rising band Los Angeles has seen in ages. The Crue's seemingly unstoppable momentum has been the result of a fortuitous combination of all six of the necessary ingredients — luck, looks, compatibility, brains, talent . . . and money.

Sure, one could complain that the band doesn't display anything that hasn't been heard or seen before, since most of their fans are too young to remember the New York Dolls, the original Sweet, and Alice Cooper in his heyday. But it really doesn't matter whether the group breaks any new ground or not. The bottom line is this: there were nothing but post-show smiles on the faces of the drained fans leaving the club.

From the opening chords of Motley's anthem, "Take Me To The Top," the band and fans tuned in to the same wavelength of raw energy, proving that the walls of the Country Club could withstand anything short of California falling into the sea. While guitarist Mick Mars stood by a lighted podium cranking out loud, rude, and aggressive power chords, and drummer Tommy Lee powered the band with his manic drumming, bassist Nikki Sixx and vocalist Vince Neal covered every inch of the stage. In addition to the band's flashy attire, the show was enhanced by an equally glitzy stage set-up, a well-choreographed light show, and a slew of Sixx originals that prove that there's more to the Crue than just an image. The Motley music ranged from the pop of "Merry Go Round" to the driving hard rock of "Come On and Dance." The most powerful songs of the night were show stoppers "Piece of Your Action," which featured some refreshingly raunchy slide guitar work by Mick Mars, and "Live Wire," which closed out the set with a blast of raw metallic power. The band probably could have played more than the three encores they did play, but now Motley Crue will find out if the rest of the world will respond to them the way their home base does.

The Crue was preceded by two long-time fixtures of the LA hard rock scene, A La Carte and Wolfgang, who hammered out two tight sets of blues-based rock for the impatient audience.
— *Stu Simone*

Vince Neal of Motley Crue. Photo: Jeff Sergent/ Tom Jamison

Act Five Mötley Crüe Go To Hell

'I'm not sure Edmonton (Canada) is ready for us yet' – Nikki Sixx, June 1982

AT WHICH point one Tom Zutaut enters the picture, shuffling on smartly, stage left. Currently in the A&R ranks at Geffen Records, Los Angeles, back in the heart of '82 he was earning his crust a little farther down the road in the marketing department at Elektra, doing whatever needed to be done in that post by day and pursuing an unofficial A&R career undercover of the night. With wetted finger aloft, he'd test out the climate at local gigs then report directly back to Joe Smith (the chairman of Elektra at the time), keeping the man at the top comprehensively in touch with goings-on at the bottom. He had a lot to say, except on one particular day when, wild of eye and red of face, he rushed frantically into the chairman's office with only *two* words to impart. In his keyed up condition they weren't all that easy to get out but eventually, after a brief lie down and a strong cup of tea, he managed it; the Big Man pressed an ear to his lips, still trembling slightly, and all was revealed . . . Mötley Crüe . . . the message had been delivered.

'What happened was, I was driving down Sunset Boulevard one day when I saw a window display for the band's first Leathür Records album and their picture just grabbed my attention,' recalls Tom, 'then two days later they played at The Whisky and I went along to check them out. After seeing 200 kids just going *crazy*, I knew I had to get them signed . . .'

It took a while, however, as these things tend to do, during which time Tom kept his identity and interest a secret from the band, but at last Joe Smith was persuaded and an offer put on the table; not as good an offer as the Virgin one, it seems, but with Elektra being a locally based company, the practical advantages of signing up with them were clear . . . the deed was done.

All things considered, the Spring of '82 was a good time for the Mötley camp: the band played a show at the Glendale Civic Auditorium on N. Verdugo (Friday, May 7) and clinched the major record deal that their forward progress depended on. So far, so good. Elektra had put its money (not to mention reputation) behind Tom Zutaut's mouth; the big question now was what would happen next?

WELL, NIKKI was in no doubt as to what *he* wanted: to press on and record a second LP with a proper producer in a proper studio with a proper budget. The Crüe's first single and album had been a tearaway success, a triumph of talent and commitment over strictly limited means, and now surely was the time to build on that. To sweep boldly forward with the financial blessing of Elektra and fashion a record bigger, better (and grosser)

65

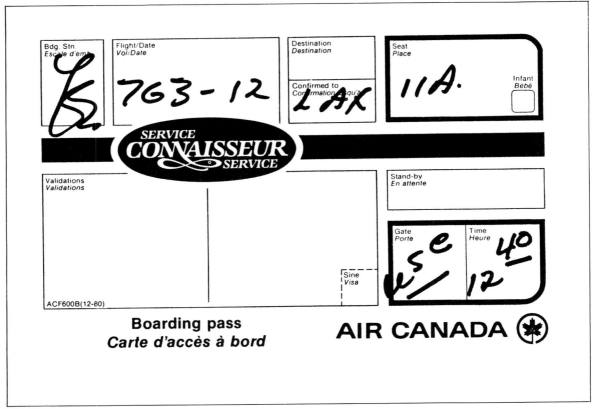

The boarding pass shows:

Bdg. Stn. / Escale d'emb [signature]
Flight/Date / Vol/Date 763-12
Destination / Destination LAX
Confirmed to / Confirmation acqu'à
Seat / Place 11A.
Infant / Bébé

SERVICE
CONNAISSEUR
SERVICE

Validations / Validations
Stand-by / En attente
Gate / Porte se/
Time / Heure 12 40
Sine / Visa

ACF600B(12-80)

Boarding pass
Carte d'accès à bord

AIR CANADA ✳

Vince's boarding pass for the ill-fated tour of Canada, the Crue's first trek outside California in June '82.

than the last, a reward for loyal fans and a vindication of a generally supportive European press. Well, that's what the bassist wanted, anyway; the company (an old, old story) had different ideas. Namely, to stop the *Too Fast For Love* LP coming out on Leathür and re-issue it in a re-mixed, slightly re-recorded form themselves. A little pointless, perhaps, a case of marking time when straight ahead seemed the obvious way to go, but history will show that that's exactly what happened . . . eventually. First, however, the band had certain outstanding commitments that needed to be honoured. A tour of Western Canada, for example . . .

From Allan Coffman's point of view the excursion North made a great deal of sense; it was a chance for the four to gain necessary road experience, to make their mistakes (if any were to be made) a few steps removed from the spotlight and, above all, it gave eight idle hands something positive to do. Left to their own devices in Los Angeles with little to occupy mind or body, Nikki and co were capable of

causing havoc wherever music was played and alcohol consumed. I mean, they're not exactly angels out on the road, being particularly keen on setting fire to hotel room doors (seldom their own) with lighter fluid and a match, but at least there's always someone on tour to carry them away to safety when things get a little *too*, uh, hot. Back home in LA, however, well . . .

'We just used to get completely out of our heads every night,' says Nikki, a hardened raiser of hell and hair, 'which didn't help matters as far as getting hassled by the police was concerned. We'd get drunk at 7.30 pm and then go out and get more drunk, and we were constantly getting into fights. We felt we had to prove ourselves, I guess.'

Answer? Take off for sunny Canada. The fresh air, the Mounties, the cry of the friendly moose, surely here, protected by the guardians of the Great White North, the Crüe could stifle destructive urges and discover internal peace. It would be the making of them . . . or, quite possibly, the death.

WHEN, SUBSEQUENT to the tour, a WEA Records spokesman admitted that, yes, 'Mötley Crüe *did* have their problems in Canada,' he may well have been making the grossest understatement in the history of

record company bullshit. Simply, had the band's first trek outside California (in June '82) been captured by a film crew it would undoubtedly have ranked alongside such bad news blockbusters as *The Towering Inferno* and *The Poseidon Adventure*. Things started off poorly and from there it was pretty much downhill all the way . . .

The four elected to make the trip North by plane, leaving their luggage to follow in a truck along with the roadies. Vince, however, forgot to include his bags so they had to travel on the seat beside him, with the result that in the course of the inevitable customs search at Edmonton airport Canuck officials were confronted with what might easily have been a porno salesman's S&M samples – whips and chains, studdedbelts, spiked wristbands, the usual stuff, all intended for stage use and all perfectly innocent, yet promptly confiscated as 'deadly weapons'. Altogether, the band were delayed for three and a half hours, during which time they were forced to relinquish around 2000 dollars-worth of spare gear along with well-thumbed copies of *Playboy* and *Hustler*, despite the fact that both are openly on sale at Canadian news-stands.

'There are probably customs

officials beatin' their wives right now with my whips and shit,' Vince told Raj Bahadur in *Scene* magazine (January 26-February 1 1984).

'Yeah, but we didn't have any drugs with us,' adds Nikki, and I should think not too . . .

'We did all those before we got off the plane!'

As for the roadbound crew, well they fared little better – *worse*, in fact, finding themselves delayed for seven hours at Couts on the Canadian border, while guards searched and re-searched for the contraband they felt sure must be there. It wasn't. For some strange reason neither Crüe nor crew felt welcome in the land of the lumberjack, and this was just the start – the visit swiftly changing from the 'Crüesing Through Canada' to the 'I'm In Hell' tour '82.

Talking to the *Union Daily* (November 19 1982), Nikki touched on some of the problems . . .

'We'd lined everything up ourselves through this agency,' he explained to Dan St. Ledger, 'and they guaranteed us 1700-seat halls to 8000-seat halls depending on whether we were supporting an act like Rainbow or Cheap Trick. But by the time we got there, there were no such places to play, so we booked into, let's say, on a Hollywood level, The Troubadour and down . . . With no pre-promotion, however, nobody knew we were coming to town. Nobody knew what to expect. It was a complete disaster.'

Complete but not immediate. The first two shows, in Lloydminster Alberta (The Wayside June 4) and Saskatoon Saskatchewan (Centennial Auditorium June 5), dragged a few locals over to the Mötley side of the tracks, and in Saskatoon there was even talk of 'five encores', but as soon as the band entered Edmonton Alberta it was clear that the good times had rolled clean away. They were booked into Scandals discotheque

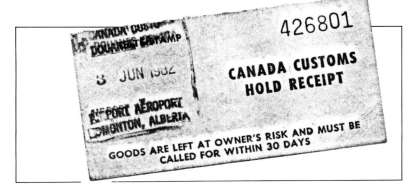

at the downtown Sheraton Caravan Hotel for a three-night stint (Monday-Wednesday, June 7/8/9), and really the name alone should have told them that this might not be their kind of place. A 180-seat new wave dance club with vaguely gay overtones, it most certainly wasn't . . .

ON TUESDAY June 8 at about 10.30pm city police rushed the Crüe members from the Scandals boards after somebody had called the station and threatened to 'waste the band on-stage'. Clearly, the four were making a few enemies in this neck of the woods; already Tommy had received a phone call from a guy who, having seen the group perform the previous night, was now threatening to blow up the hotel and all the guests along with it. Thus, the boys in blue escorted the troupe safely upstairs – they'd taken over the whole eighth floor of the Sheraton – and began to conduct a search.

'They made us stay in the elevators and they took our keys and checked every single room,' the *Edmonton Journal* quoted Coffman as saying, and though nothing was uncovered, two policemen stood vigil at the side of the stage for the rest of the evening's performance, one of them apparently sporting earplugs!

And as for the Monday night (June 7), well that had been no picnic

either. An intrepid Graham Hicks from the *Edmonton Sun* had witnessed the band play and was quite impressed – 'Good, hard rock . . . teenage anthem stuff', he wrote – though the same couldn't be said for the majority of the crowd. According to Hicks, 'the wavish element in Scandals would have booed Van Halen. By intermission, hardly a hand struck another in the club . . . this could be history in the making. Mötley Crüe's lowest moment.'

A moment witnessed, strangely enough, by bassist Rudy Sarzo and keyboard man Don Airey, both part of the Ozzy Osbourne Band at the time and in town to do their bit at the Coliseum.

'Yeah, they came to see us play,' recalls Vince. 'We stuffed stacks of equipment into this little bar and the people in the audience just didn't know what to make of us at all. They threw bottles (a beer bottle cut Nikki's right hand open – 'I just threw blood on the crowd and kept playing!') and while we were taking a break – we had to play four sets – some guy came backstage and made a comment to Tommy. He was ready to take a swing at him but Allan Coffman grabbed the guy, took him by the head and bashed his teeth in with his knee. He used to be an MP in Vietnam and he was a cop in '69 in San Francisco; he's a pretty tough guy!'

The Crüe managed to escape from that situation but the tide was clearly against them: Coffman broke a finger in defence of their honour, a planned live broadcast of part of the evening's performance by radio station CKRA K-97 was scuttled due to the ruckus, and had it not been for a degree of coaxing from the gentlemanly Mr Sarzo, the band might not have gone back on-stage at all. Vince, by this point, was seriously fired up.

'Since we've been in your country,' he told the audience, 'we've been in fights, had threats on our lives and had our stage clothes taken away.

• The Edmonton Sun, Thursday, June 10, 1982 **27**

MOTLEY SHOW GOES ON BUT...

Death threats worry band

But we're still gonna show you how to rock, Los Angeles style, and if you don't like it fuck you!'

Half expecting to end up as a human sacrifice, Hicks manfully sought out the group at the end of the evening for a brief comment on events, instantly stopping an earful from an adrenalised Nikki, bloody but unbowed . . .

'We're a concert band!' he hollered, 'this stage wouldn't normally take care of our drum-kit. Everywhere else we've been we've had three encores. As a rule, we carry thirty-two smoke bombs and we're going to be huge because we're entertainment. Our next album will be called *TV And Violence* (a 'psychopathic' song that Nikki still has tucked firmly up his sleeve). We're the television. Our audience is the violence. Together we'll take over the world!!!'

Yes . . . Vince, however, was a little more restrained . . .

'It's been great for our egos,' he commented, 'knocked us down about five notches.'

The band finished their stint at Scandals the next night, then, complete with an emergency police number, moved on to another part of Edmonton for shows at the Riviera Rock Room on the Thursday and Friday (June 10/11). At least this place sounded a little more promising, though before the Crüe could get *too* excited they were rudely brought back down to earth, finding the manager of the Sheraton and two bodyguards laying in wait for them at the venue, the trio demanding payment of a 260 dollar bill for the alleged 'trashing' of the hotel's eighth floor.

'That's a pretty cheap eighth floor,' observed Nikki with a chuckle (particularly as the four seemed to have organised a competition to see whose Sony TV would hit the pavement first, Tommy coming out on top with a killer time of five seconds precisely!)

In the end, the band paid for damage to a lamp, a couple of door knobs, several goose-down pillows and other assorted items, enabling the Riviera gigs to go ahead; indeed, the second night a live broadcast finally went out on K-97, though by this stage, devoid of record company support and with fate doing them no service whatsoever, the Crüe were perilously close to deciding that enough was (more than) enough. When they were refused entry into British Columbia, the remaining dozen or so dates were considered not to be worth the trouble and the four returned

gratefully to the altogether greener pastures of LA – though not before Vince had sent the press clippings screaming about bomb and death threats home to his mother. The note attached was a simple one. It read: 'having a good time . . .'

ON JULY 22/23, a Thursday/Friday, Mötley Crüe played two sell-out nights at The Country Club, an achievement which must have helped to erase any mental scars left over from the aborted Canadian jaunt (the promoter of that jaunt, incidentally, has now decided that he would very much like to sue the band for a million dollars – the inevitable price of success). It was good to be home, and on August 20 Elektra re-issued the *Too Fast For Love* album, this third fooled-around-with version of the LP eventually going gold in the US (500,000 copies sold) and, ironically, gold in Canada too (50,000 copies sold).

Some of the changes made to the Leathür Records original were purely cosmetic – the enlargement of the logo on the front cover, the reduction of the photos on the rear, the re-shuffling of the tracks and the addition of a new OTT photo on the inner bag – but others (unfortunately) went a great deal deeper, gnawing away at the vinyl itself . . .

The truth is, the powers that be at Elektra really weren't too sure *what* to make of this signing; they walked round them, eyed them up and down, viewed them from every possible angle and then, in a flash of desperation, decided that obvious rough edges were probably the area in need of most attention. There wasn't much that could be done with the band themselves, of course (I mean, these guys were never *ever* gonna look like labelmates Jackson Browne or the Eagles, and as for Linda Ronstadt . . .), but their record could certainly be smoothed down a little; more polish and less spit, a touch of oil on troubled waters, it had all been done before and who better to administer the gloss than famed producer Roy Thomas Baker, a man linked with names such as Queen, Journey and The Cars.

'Paint a garbage can platinum and it's still a garbage can,' is Nikki's hindsight comment on 'operation clean-up', but the record company had the bit between its teeth and was determined not to be halted. Vince, it was felt, should completely redo some of his vocal parts, to which end he was originally going to break off briefly from the Canadian tour and fly home to LA, but with the

entire band returning far sooner than expected anyway, getting him back into the studio proved no great problem. Doubtless experiencing a certain sense of *deja vu*, the singer did all that was asked of him one more time with feeling, after which 'Stick to Your Guns' was removed from the album to improve overall sound quality (a democratic band selection, though Nikki would someday like to re-record the song) and the whole package re-mixed by Gordon Fordyce at Cherokee Studios, Hollywood, with RTB in supreme supervisory control.

All well and good certainly, or at least it would be if I'd ever met anyone, Mötley Crüe fan or not, who prefers the re-mix to the original version. The band definitely don't . . .

'Elektra just tried to make us more accessible to the radio,' says Vince, 'it sounded *way* cooler before they messed with it.'

Nikki agrees. 'It doesn't have enough r .uts!' he told Xavier Russell (*Kerrang!* issue 30, December 2-15 1982), getting straight to the crutch, uh, *crux* of the problem, and despite the extra attention paid to the drum sound it has to be said that he's right. Completely.

IT WAS the same old tale of woe. Once again the Crüe found themselves mishandled by people – well-meaning, perhaps – who just didn't, or couldn't comprehend what they were all about. Which is? Well, according to Nikki, the vital ingredients are 'sex, drugs, pizza and more sex', with pizza I understand something of an optional extra, 'we're intellectuals on a crotch level. We're the guys in High School your parents warned you to stay away from. That's what we're like on-stage and off. The kids won't buy albums from phonies. They can see right through that crap. They'll run your ass out of the country if you aren't the real thing!'

Mötley Crüe *are* the real thing, 'the extremly real thing', to quote

**Opposite: Elektra Records'
version of the** *TFFL* **LP . . . and
above: the new pic that appeared
in the inner bag.**

Nikki, yet initially at least, Elektra
would clearly have been happier
with a surrogate, a more cautious
carbon copy.

At this point, it would be very easy
indeed to slip into the world of the
cliché; to paint a two-dimensional
portrait of the corporate, dollar-
conscious record company pulling
the impoverished artist this way and
that until his face (and the rest) fits
easily into a pre-determined
pigeon-hole. That you've no doubt
heard a hundred times before –
which doesn't mean to say it isn't
true, just boring – so suffice it to say
here that by this stage Mötley Crüe
were feeling more than a touch
frustrated. Signed or unsigned, they

just couldn't seem to win, and the
behaviour of their manager wasn't
helping matters either . . .

At first things had been OK, the
two parties learning together side
by side yet remaining ignorant
enough not to recognise the
impossible; the band had moved
from point A to point B and now
needed to make that all-important
jump to high C . . . which is where
Coffman's sense of direction started
to fail him. Locally, he knew every
twist and turn, but out in the big bad
world it was an altogether different
story. Says Vince:

'I think Allan helped us as much
as he could, but it all got too
overwhelming for him. We became
too big too fast and he just kinda
freaked. Actually, he built up a
reputation for himself as the biggest
jerk around, he really did. He had no
respect in the music business and

that hurt us – I think he blew a lot of
deals; without him we'd probably
have been signed much sooner.
Also, we found out that he was doing
certain things with our money that he
shouldn't . . .'

Without delving too deep into the
dirt, it became obvious to the band
that all was not as it should be when,
despite selling out big local shows,
they found they didn't even have the
money for a new pair of shoes! They
were coming away with very little
and the road crew likewise – even
though Coffman had already
received an advance from the
record company to get 'his boys' out
on the road in support of their *TFFL*
LP. Where was it all going? The
Crüe weren't sure (but they had
more than a fair idea), and to make
matters worse it wasn't unusual for
Coffman to arrange for a gig to be
recorded live for radio broadcast

without so much as a word in their direction. 'Come on! You didn't need to know *that* . . .' the situation was completely out of hand . . .

'Allan Coffman was a man with a very good heart,' says Nikki calmly, 'but when we got the record deal with Elektra he started to become greedy and take us for granted – that's why we had to part company with him. He didn't spend a lot of money really 'cos we always paid him back after every gig. We always kept even with him.'

With Coffman's hold relinquished (he now appears to have bowed graciously out of the music industry), it was time to sit down and get the future into perspective. Nikki, as ever, saw things in strictly black and white terms, vowing with hand on nearest Cheap Trick album that Mötley Crüe would either go on to become one of the biggest, most successful bands in the history of rock'n'roll or else bust clean apart at the seams. It was all or nothing, entertainment or death, the familiar Mötley cry, and there was no question at all that it came straight from the heart . . .

Act Sixx Leaving home ('Tulsa, Oklahoma, are you ready to rock?!')

'Prediction: "There will be complete mayhem and destruction". Resolution: "Mötley Crüe will help bring this about in 1983" - Nikki Sixx' (*BAM* December 26 1982).
AT 9.00PM on New year's Eve 1982, Mötley Crüe played to a sell-out crowd at the Santa Monica Civic, a concert promoted by LA radio station KMET 94.7 and Avalon Attractions. It was the culmination of what, in local gigging terms at least, had been a highly successful year for the band; from the previously mentioned Glendale Civic Auditorium (May 7) to The Roxy Theatre (Friday/Saturday, September 24/25, supported by Steeler and Sharks respectively), the troupe had kept audiences permanently on their toes, and at *really* busy shows on each others! For the kids it was a chance to dress up and act cool, to pose and to pester, like Halloween every night – especially come October and a show at the Concord Pavilion, San Francisco, when it *was* Halloween! Just for *one* night, of course (the 31st), but then quantity ain't everything . . .
    In front of 9000 people, sandwiched between Randy Hansen and Y&T at an outdoor amphitheatre, the Crüe put on a performance described by Xavier Russell (*Kerrang!* issue 30, December 2-15 1982) as 'perhaps the greatest glam rock show of all time'. The skulls and the stakes, the voodoo vibe and the lavish use of pyro, it was all too much for the man and something of a shock to both Y&T and the attendant fire marshall (whose last words to the four had expressly forbidden the use of anything more potent than a heavily dampened sparkler). Spoil-sport tactics, I'm afraid, and the band had always found a finger for those in the past so why should this occasion be

any different? Indeed, as far as Mötley were concerned, this seemed an ideal opportunity to tear down all barriers (metaphorically speaking . . . I think) and come on strong with a selection of their choicest moves – to revive their 'no smoke without fire' routine, a firm favourite with authorities everywhere (I don't think) and fire marshalls in particular.
    'I had this sword that I'd wave around with a turpentine gel on it,' explains Vince, 'then I'd touch it to a candelabra in front of the stacks and it would go up in flames. While I was doing all this, Nikki would run to the side of the stage where someone was ready to cover his boots with the same stuff, after which I'd touch them with the sword and he'd go up in flames too. I'd also touch the back of his guitar, which again had the gel on it, so he'd walk out to the front with his guitar and boots on fire . . . we got fined 1000 dollars as soon as we came off-stage that night!'
    An eventful outing certainly, though the Crüe's New Year's Eve performance was altogether more significant: dubbed the 'New Year's Evil' show and representing just about every cent the four had between them, it was either to be their last time on stage 'neath the Mötley banner or else a genuine watershed in the band's career. They'd either close their case with a

crash, a bang and a bloody great wallop or else convert record company apathy and take it all the way to the top, the key to the latter course being a fresh management set-up designed to make them happenin' rather than hungry . . .
    'It really was a do or die situation,' recalls Vince, ''cos we couldn't manage ourselves. We'd had a lot of offers from different people but no-one seemed right. They wanted this or that, y'know . . .'
    'So we called every manager we'd ever heard of and invited them along to the Santa Monica Civic for what was probably one of the best New Year's Eve shows there's ever been. We had twenty foot high mortars going off and a chainsaw – it was *wild*! We used to have this styrofoam dummy that looked like Wendy O. Williams and we'd put these rubbers filled with blood inside the neck, which was already cut off – there was just a wooden pole in the centre to keep it in place.'
    'Anyway, this guy in a mask would drag it out on-stage in chains, at which point I'd start up the chainsaw, cut off the head – the blood would just spurt *everywhere!* – and hold it up. I'd put on my Crüe hard hat for that . . .'
    Very sensible.
    I'm not too sure what the collective term for rock managers is (a 'percentage' perhaps) but

ROXY THEATRE

9009 SUNSET BLVD. 276-2222

SEPTEMBER 24, 25
HELL'S REVENGE FROM THE BOYS
YOU LOVE TO HATE
Mötley Crüe
24TH STEELER
25TH SHARKS

surveying this spectacle from the relative safety of the audience were some of the top names in the business, taking up the invitation to come along and cast an eye. Cliff Bernstein, for example, current co-manager of Def Leppard, Dokken, Metallica and Armored Saint, rubbing his chin thoughtfully alongside David Krebs from CCC (Contemporary Communications Corporation), the Scorpions present US manager and one-time associate of Ted Nugent and Aerosmith, not to mention former Kiss adviser Bill Aucoin, taken back perhaps to August 10 1973 and a seedy ballroom in Manhattan where he first set eyes on another four-man outfit heavy on the make-up and the mayhem. He was interested, it seems, as were the rest, though the early part of the evening might just have thrown them a touch off keel, their balance seriously tested in the crosswinds of confusion . . .

For this make-or-break performance, time to stand up and be counted or simply counted out, Nikki wasn't going to settle for any old support act. Oh no. Imagination locked into overdrive and light-bulb flashing crazily overhead, he snapped his fingers and before him appeared the misty vision of a

rock'n'roll circus, a carnival of incandescent colour and crunching chords. It was all there, hurtling through hoops inside his head, and when Nikki gets a yearning to do something . . .

Thus, the early arrivals at the New Year's Eve show were greeted not by the usual third-on-the-billers attempting to drag something approaching a favourable response from an audience still digesting its first drink (or three), but by gypsies and jugglers, a smell-of-the-greasepaint atmosphere and . . . a punk band called The Wigglers! Well, it was novel anyway, the sort of stunt that either goes down a storm or else winds up a complete and utter disaster, instantly hated by all with the power to see and hear . . . The kids *hated* it – particularly The Wigglers – though some might have been a little peeved at the banning of a scheduled 'Miss Nude Heavy Metal' contest by the Santa Monica authorities, perhaps on grounds of bad taste or perhaps, as *Calendar* reported (Sunday, January 9 1983), because many of the contestants were 'too young to appear on-stage in such an unusual beauty pageant'. Simply, it was left to Mötley Crüe to revive the evening, which they did with considerable success – this

was backyard territory, after all. They'd already played two packed-out Friday night shows at Perkins Palace in November and they had no problem icing that particular cake come New Year's Eve.

Doc McGhee, then Pat Travers manager who'd been told about the event by his attorney, was certainly entertained. The band were new and unpolished, no doubt about that, teetering around apparently on the brink of collapse, their music stalking that fine line 'twixt sloppiness and spontaneity, yet the basic ingredients for success were clearly present – a little jumbled, perhaps, but present nonetheless. Potential is the word, a word that refused to budge from the tip of the McGhee tongue until the Crüe had concluded matters in traditional style with their 'Helter Skelter' encore. He was hooked . . .

'Actually, I was taking my girlfriend to the Cayman Islands (in the West Indies) for a vacation,' he recalls, 'but we flew in for the show at Santa Monica and when I saw the group I went "that's it!" I knew then that they'd probably be the biggest

act in the world. It happened that quickly . . . when you see 3500 kids standing there shouting and buying up every piece of merchandise there is, you don't have to be a rocket scientist to figure out what the band can do if you clean it up and show it off to the rest of the world. Every concert I've done I've been impressed by the response of the fans; whether the guys played good or bad, the kids were with them all the time.'

MÖTLEY CRÜE inked the dotted line with McGhee Enterprises Inc (in effect, Doc and associate Doug Thaler, formerly with the Leber/ Krebs organisation) in February 1983, having flown to Las Vegas on Doc's private plane to hang out for a while and see how he ran his organisation. Needless to say, they were as impressed watching him in action as he'd been watching them, feeling that here was a man unlikely to book them gigs in gay Canadian discos. They wanted to play to *real* rock'n'roll audiences, not 'cowboys with tattoos of anchors on their arms that said "mom" '; kids who take their music heavy and their bands bad of ass and high of hair; kids who like the theatrical touch; a Kiss audience perhaps . . .

On March 26 1983 at the 5700- capacity Irvine Meadows Amphitheatre, Laguna Hills, California, Mötley Crüe played the first of five major shows – a genuine tour at last! – opening up for a legendary New York act. The act in question: Kiss. The motto of the tour: every man to his own mascara!

For Tommy, the gigs were a particular buzz – if a little weird. Before he got the chance to do damage to a proper drum-kit, it seems that he'd improvised quite successfully on pots and pans and cardboard boxes, even the wall and the floor, accompanying the beat behind two particular records: one by the Osmonds, the album featuring 'Crazy Horses', and the other the first self-titled *Kiss* LP, 'Firehouse' being his favourite song at the time.

That was 1974. Almost 10 years later, with make-up still intact and 'Firehouse' still in the set (both subsequently dropped, of course), the Kiss shows jogged his memory and filled in a few missing gaps . . .

'I remember when the guys from the band walked in to do their soundcheck; I'd never seen them without make-up before and I went "wow!" I'm looking at Gene Simmons and going "I didn't know he looked like *that*!" '

For their 'Creatures Of The Night'

tour, a return to road duties after three years out of favour, Kiss' choice of support band certainly extended a good many eyebrows – in an *upward* direction. Already they'd taken out the Plasmatics, an outfit not exactly known for its sobriety, and now Mötley Crüe, a group being openly compared to them in almost every quarter. To some they were shamefaced copyists, to others clear successors, though Nikki really couldn't see how the two names had ever come to be linked.

Sure, both parties had a hand firmly lodged in the make-up jar, but in terms of music and presentation he reckoned the differences to be substantial. And then, of course, there was attitude. The Crüe were lean and pushing for success, whereas Kiss . . . well, they'd been there before, all the way, so perhaps the ball was in the underdog's court. The frontline correspondents certainly seemed to think so and, after the remainder of the shows in Universal City (March 27), Phoenix (March 28), Las Vegas (April 1) and San Francisco (April 3), strong areas for the LA mob, Nikki too was in little doubt . . .

'Y'know, I like Kiss a lot,' he explains, 'and there's no question that they're hungry again now – that happened when they took off the make-up – but when we toured together they were really just going through the motions. It was like, here comes the tongue, here comes the fire, OK Paul (Stanley) jump, let's play another hit!'

FROM THE standpoint of experience and exposure, the Kiss dates definitely proved useful for the Crüe. In Phoenix they opened up proceedings in a 10,000-seater (The Veterans Memorial Auditorium) and the venue in San Francisco (The Civic Auditorium) has been known to house up to 8000 cheering rock fans 'neath its rafters, yet neither of these two showings, prestigious though they may have been, in any way prepared them for what was to come – the next step up the ladder. I guess you could call it a *biggie* . . .

'They came in cars. They came on foot (when the cars boiled over in the 95 degree heat, inching along the endless line from the San Bernadino Freeway to the searchpoint). 600,000 people over a three-day weekend called the US Festival. 300,000 or more for the heavy metal day alone.'

So wrote Laura Canyon in *Kerrang!* (issue 46, July 14-27), braving the dust and the smog to report on the festival that, more than

anything else, represented a triumph for the world of heavy rock, making it clear to one and all – the American music industry in particular – just how popular the hard stuff really is. Organised by Unuson and more specifically Steve Wozniak, head of the massive Apple computer company and self- confessed non-HM fan, the event just about had it all: on the less than pleasant side, 130 arrests, one murder (over a drugs deal) and a few bloody bodies, but overwhelming the negative aspects was a whole plethora of plusses – acrobats, hot-air balloons, a reasonable twenty dollar ticket price, giant video screens and something, in theory at least, to suit most musical tastes.

Day one (May 28 1983) went ahead under a 'new music' banner, with Men At Work's performance being beamed live to the Soviet Union who in turn beamed back a snippet of one of their own jazz-fusion bands Arsenal, and headline act the Clash getting into a scrap with the organisers. Day three (May 30) was devoted to more mainstream rock: David Bowie topped the bill, his first Stateside appearance in five years, backed up by the likes of Joe Walsh and the Pretenders, but, according to those roasting on the spot, it was day two (May 29), heavy metal day, that had both the biggest turnout and the headiest festival atmosphere.

'The American Experience: here it is!' one reporter commented and Laura Canyon agreed, going on to speak of 'guys peeling off their leather and eyeing cute young girls in tiny bikinis and high-heeled shoes . . . there really was a love vibe out there. Everyone on HM day *adored* every band on the bill'.

Who were they? Local boys Quiet Riot, Ozzy Osbourne, Judas Priest, Triumph, the Scorpions, headliners Van Halen (apparently granted a million dollars for a two hour show!) . . . *and* Mötley Crüe, second into the fray after Quiet Riot and scheduled to hit the 435-foot-wide stage at high noon (or should that be high *at* noon?), the sort of unholy hour when most self-respecting rockers are just easing bones between sheets after a hard night on the brew. Nikki normally allows himself five shots of whisky per gig (no drugs) and he certainly needed them all for this one, the band effectively playing what will probably remain the biggest show of their career: a US tour in one swoop and on limited rehearsal time too . . .

'The audience was as loud as the

PA system,' Nikki told Mark Lundahl from the *San Bernadino Sun* (November 4 1983), 'it was really wild!'

'We were all just freaking out,' adds Tommy, 'and what made it rougher was the heat. It was very dusty and hard to breath – I almost passed out!'

And then there was Mick, who had problems all his own. Being of pale complexion, it certainly didn't suit him to play under the midday sun, particularly in oil-based stage make-up, but the show had to go on so there was little he could do aside from grin and bear it. Or rather *not* bare it, covering up as much as a rock star can and still be considered C.O.O.L. And Vince? Well, like the rest of the band he tried to pace himself, but by the time he got to 'Live Wire' with its singalonga Crüe section the heat and the dust had finally taken their toll, making vocal high jinx both difficult and dangerous. Not easy, y'see, though braving the Sahara conditions and shaking a fist at the Heavens certainly upped the group's reputation; indeed, Nikki has the festival mentally marked down as the first occasion on which Mötley Crüe were recognised as a *serious* musical force. Besides which, it provided an invaluable opportunity to air fresh material.

Already they'd let a few things slip from their sleeve at the Halloween show – 'Looks That Kill', 'Shout At The Devil', 'Red Hot' – but now was the time for a more extensive unveiling. To the majority of the crowd the new numbers were exactly that(new), but they still managed to join in come chorus time, tossing back heads and punching hard into the steamy air. Later down the line the songs would come under the pre-production hammer of Tom Werman, at which point a certain amount of tidying up and brushing down would inevitably take place. At this stage though, the material was still wet off the easel – original arrangements intact and lyrics untampered with – something that makes the 'Devil's Best Friends' bootleg of the band's festival appearance a genuine collector's item.

Next stop: the studio.
SHOUT AT THE DEVIL, the second Mötley Crüe LP, was put out in America by Elektra Records on September 26 1983, gaining a European release the following month. Produced by the aforementioned Tom Werman (of Ted Nugent/Cheap Trick infamy), a paternal figure known to the band as

'dad', and recorded/mixed by Geoff Workman with Doug Schwartz acting as second engineer, it represented the band's first properly organised entry into the world of recording. Everything else, including demo tapes of new songs put together after the *Too Fast For Love* LP, had been handled production-wise (and in all other aspects) by the group themselves in time-saving fashion. But now, with a major like Elektra dishing out the dollars, they could afford to stretch out a little more, work a sensible recording schedule in a top LA studio (Cherokee, Hollywood) and select their material with care.

In fact, they had a whole bunch of songs to pick from: 'Shout At The Devil', 'Looks That Kill', 'Knock 'Em Dead, Kid', 'Red Hot', 'Helter Skelter', numbers that easily made the transition from live set to record, as well as others that didn't. And there was some good stuff that didn't: 'Run For Your Life', 'Survive', 'Running Wild In The Night', all pretty classy, though the band weren't too struck on the verses of the latter and have now transplanted the lyrics (with suitable amendments) onto 'Save Our Souls', track three side two of the *Theatre Of Pain* album.

Perhaps the most surprising exclusion, however, was a Sixx-penned song called 'The Black Widow', a quite stunning slow-burner recorded in the same demo session as 'Shout . . .' and significant for its inclusion of the line *'In this theatre of pain, love and hate's the same,'* clearly a foretaste of future goings-on. Latest word on this front is that the number may eventually surface on the soundtrack to a movie; Nikki discussed the idea with Gene Simmons in a Beverly Hills hotel room earlier this year and would seem to have former Hanoi Rocks frontman Mike Monroe in mind as a possible vocalist, but so far no more definite news has come to light. We'll see . . .

Still, that said, there was no arguing with the ten compositions that finally found their way onto the LP. In addition to those already mentioned there was 'Bastard', dedicated to Allan Coffman and containing the clenched-fist couplet *'Get on your knees, please beg me, please/You're the king of the sleaze, don't you try to rape me'*; 'Danger', a Sixx-eye view of Hollywood, the city of (broken) dreams, that reduced Tom Zutaut to tears the first time he heard it; 'Looks That Kill', the first American single, and 'Too Young To Fall In Love', the second (released January '84 and April '84

respectively); 'Ten Seconds To Love', about 'quickie sex in an elevator'; and the haunting instrumental 'God Bless The Children Of The Beast', recorded one and all on 'Foster's Lager, Budweiser, Bombay Gin, lots of Jack Daniels, Kahlua and Brandy, Quackers and Krell, and wild women!' I don't know if the order here is of any significance, but I'm sure that each one played its part – to the max!

One section of the album not yet mentioned, however, is the very beginning, a narrative, scene-setting passage called – appropriately enough – 'In The Beginning'. Nikki came up with the words but didn't deliver the speech, that honour falling (if the sleeve notes are to be trusted) to longstanding band mascot Allister Fiend, a mythical character with certain Eddie-like overtones. He hadn't made it onto vinyl before, but to Crüe fans he was far from an alien figure and to the group themselves an old and intimate friend. Nikki was even there at his birth . . .

'It was hilarious,' he recalls, 'we just went down to a theatrical shop and bought a skull mask then persuaded one of our roadies to come on-stage wearing it; it was kinda like a Grim Reaper figure. Anyway, he'd appear amidst all this smoke and mime to a tape of somebody reciting 'The Conquerer Worm' (a poem by Edgar Allan Poe containing the line "That motley drama-oh, be sure/It shall not be forgot!'), we took it from a record and put it onto tape, then we'd come on-stage and open up the show. We called that character Allister Fiend, a cross between Alistair Crowley and the idea of a fiend.'

With the nature and role of Allister still being somewhat nebulous – though he did figure later on T-shirts alongside such celebrated Mötley merchandising as two-colour dayglow shirts and 'Kamikaze' headbands – Nikki toyed with the idea of using an established 'name' to deliver the intro on the record; someone who could give both life and depth to the character. Orson Welles, perhaps, who'd already lent his not inconsiderable weight to the first Manowar album, *Battle Hymns,* or a celebrated English actor in the Shakespearian mould. Noble ideas certainly, though in the end it was Geoff Workman of 'behemoth sounds' fame who was trusted with the task, getting to grips with a passage designed to clarify/unify the whole *Shout At The Devil* theme. Says Nikki:

"The idea behind the concept was

Gatefold and back cover of the *Shout At The Devil* album, released in the US in September 1983.

shouting at the things that are drawing people to their knees, like politicians. In my mind's eye, I started it in the past and brought it forward to a day when all the cities were destroyed; the only things left were "ashes of dreams" and "corpses of rebels", people who'd fought against the government and been killed.'

The LP is dedicated to 'the young and the young at heart' (as is *Theatre Of Pain,* at least in part) and 'In The Beginning' voices the belief that 'those who have the youth have the future', a concept given the ultimate in bad press through its close association with the Hitler Youth movement. Anyone who's seen the movie 'Cabaret', and in particular the angel-faced young Nazi singing 'Tomorrow Belongs To Me', will know just how sinister and spine-chilling a concept that can be. But Nikki is of the opinion that it's up to the youth to change things for the *better*; to stand tall, 'be strong and shout at the devil', the 'devil' in this sense meaning figures in authority and, more specifically, those

figures who *abuse* their positions of power and influence – bad authority holders, rotten people and rotten governments.

In this general sense, the devil might well be different things to different people. To a child it could be a violent parent, to an adolescent an unfair teacher or a corrupt policeman and to an adult a self-seeking politician, perhaps, anyone who grinds you down, dampens your spirit and slams your back against the nearest, hardest wall. If the youth really do have the future, then it's up to them, the rock fans, to change the system and bellow long and loud in the ear of corruption, and up to the *real* youth leaders of the 80's, the stars of the rock'n'pop firmament, to speak and act responsibly and make sure that they don't become the 'devils' of tomorrow, hard of hearing and solid of soul . . .

Proud idealism or ill-conceived claptrap? Brave words or bullshit? That's for the individual, *you*, to determine. But whatever you say or think, the concept clearly has nothing to do with the Devil in the traditional sense. We aren't talkin' pitch-forks or pointed tails here, though (perhaps inevitably) the whole thing was monstrously

misunderstood, drawing forth the wrath of the 'moral majority' and just about anyone with a soapbox to stand on. Ozzy had had it, Kiss (Knights In Satan's Service, it was said) had had it and now it was someone else's turn. To Nikki, Tommy, Mick and Vince, it was all too clear who that 'someone' was . . .

THE LINK between the forces of darkness and the world of heavy rock is one of both depth and duration. Black Widow, Black Sabbath, Arthur Brown, Screaming Lord Sutch, Screaming Jay Hawkins, Alice Cooper, all have dipped at least a toe into darker waters, but then that does tend to suit the nature of the beast – and, of course, its children.

It's a fact, y'see, that HM is a music of extremes, often doomy and threatening, *always* loud and usually backed up by an arsenal of special FX, a kind of dry run for the apocalypse. It's a world where tight black leather and heavy velvet cloaks blend in far easier than sharply cut suits and bright narrow ties; the world of the carefully ripped T-shirt, the Kensington Market boot and the mean, mean stare. It has its own vernacular, its own code of conduct and, as you'd expect, its own imagery – and if that

Motley Crue circa *Shout At The Devil* **with new streamlined clothes as weapons image.**

imagery does tend to focus on warts and warlocks, tastefully located in bone-crushing Bosch landscapes, then it's only because the music demands that it be so. After all, in the immortal words of Judas Priest frontman Rob Halford you 'can't really go on-stage and sing about daffodils with 40,000 watts of power.'

It isn't all this way, of course. Take a glance and you'll come across the party-orientated approach of bands like Quiet Riot, the whiter than whiteness of LA Christian rockers Stryper and the tongue-in-beard humour of ZZ Top. But I suspect that to many on the 'outside' the image most closely associated with the heavy rock sphere is the infernal one, and why should these Mötley Crüe people be any different? They've got long hair, haven't they? I mean, any band who looks like they do can't have anything to say musically, right? Can't have anything to contribute? Compositions? *De*compositions more like! Clearly, the Crüe were all flash and no substance, all outer trimmings and no inner strength, all black (hearts) and no grey (matter), yeah?

In other words, there were many who never saw beyond the pentagrams and the pouts; many

who gave the album no more than a superficial scan and came slap bang against the conclusion that the four guys pictured on the sleeve were a bunch of evil reprobates, perniciously plotting the moral destruction of the truth'n'justice seeking sons and daughters (particularly daughters) of the Great American Dreamland. Mötley Crüe? No good Devil-worshippers, right? RIGHT?!!

Well, no actually – no need for garlic here. It's true that Nikki tends to lean more towards the 'black-hat' side of things, considering it's way cooler to be the villain than the hero and that he did once succeed in getting laid in a coffin, but when it came to writing songs for the *Shout . . .* LP it was anger rather than evil that guided his hand over the frets. He's mellowed somewhat now, of course, but back in the old days you could have fried an egg on his forehead; Coffman was making all the wrong moves, Elektra weren't making *any* moves and the band felt trapped within the confines of LA. Too many hopefuls had struck it big there and nowhere else, and the Crüe were determined that it wouldn't happen to them. With the Kiss dates and the US Festival

already tucked firmly under their collective corset, along with a one-shot show with Def Leppard in San Diego on September 17 1983, the combined weight of the bill (completed by Uriah Heep and Eddie Money) drawing around 50,000 people to the football stadium home of the San Diego chargers, it was time for the four to strike out alone . . .

ON NOVEMBER 11 1983 Mötley Crüe played to a sell-out crowd at the 600-capacity Orange Pavillion, San Bernadino, the first stop on a headline tour of twenty three cities that was to take them as close to home as the Santa Monica civic (for three jam-packed nights) and as far afield as Portland Oregon, Seattle Washington, Denver Colorado, Tulsa Oklahoma, San Angelo Texas and Albuquerque New Mexico, the whole thing drawing to a close at the 200-seat Centennial Hall in Mesa Arizona on December 16. Florida outfit Axe supported on all the dates, with Australian transplants Heaven joining the bill on twelve of them, but it was the Crüe name that was shifting the tickets, there was no doubt about that; they had the look, the stageshow – an all-new futuristic construction of 'stone' and 'spikes', described by Nikki as 'a heavy metal city that's been destroyed, and we're like the heavy metal warriors' – and a lethal pyro set-up designed by Tom Hammer. Bang, bang!

Employing Doc's eight-seater Navaho Chieftain to fly between engagements, the band found themselves setting concert hall records for sales of merchandise (T-shirts, posters, wristbands and fingerless gloves) wherever they came into land; success was snapping hard at their heels and the grins were there, neon-bright, for all to see. When an electrical malfunction forced the plane into an emergency dive to the ground, causing stage make-up and cleansers to explode inside stowed away luggage, the four simply shrugged their shoulders and pressed on regardless. And when they found themselves in Denver and their equipment trucks stranded helplessly in a snowstorm in Wyoming, they just kept hold of their cool, invited Heaven and Axe down to the Holiday Inn bar and, as Nikki told Richard Hogan in *Circus* magazine (March 31 1984), 'got ripped for four days. It was a blast!'

Luck at last seemed to be on their side, though Mick probably had something choice to say about that when a few months later in Colorado springs he was carted away on a charge of indecent exposure with an eighteen year old girl. Actually, the whole thing was a ghastly mistake (no, honest!), as Nikki explains . . .

'At the time I had a fetish for sleeping in closets – I don't know why – and I was in there with some chicks while Tommy was running up and down the hallway of our hotel wearing nothing but a leather G-string. Anyway, the police were called and it was reported that Tommy had been seen diving into our room; they came to check it out but by that point he'd already left so, with me in the closet, the only person they saw with black hair was Mick. He was arrested, taken to jail and fined, but the whole thing *was* a mistake!'

Poor ol' Mick. No doubt that night in a moonlit cell another black mark against the world found its way into his (very large) black book. He wasn't having it easy, but as for Vince, well, he was too busy keeping an eye on the scenery to fall foul of the law – by accident or otherwise. Prior to the Crüe's first major headline tour – we won't count the Canadian episode, OK? – he'd travelled (within the US) as far from his LA home as Las Vegas . . . and stopped. *Dead*. With the West Coast

being so self-contained he hadn't really felt the need to visit foreign parts; it was all there on his doorstep – mountains, beaches and snow, the whole geographical gamut – yet once out on the road he started to realise exactly what he'd been missing. Nothing broadens the mind like travel, they say, so as soon as the dates were over he decided to go for broke with a two week course of mind-expansion in the Cayman Islands and Tommy, also feeling the educational urge, opted to join him . . .

It proved the perfect break; temperatures between eighty and ninety degrees and nothing much to do. Occasionally, if they felt madly energetic and just a little bit wanton, the pair would journey down to Hell, a one-horse dot on the map boasting nothing more than a post office, a gas station and the appropriately titled Club Inferno, and come New Year's Eve they successfully summoned the energy to jam with a local reggae band on 'I Shot The Sheriff' (what else?), but for the most part strenuous action was kept to a minimum. Sometimes out-lawed altogether.

It was a time for relaxing, for snuggling down in the sand and lining both senses and stomach with as much protective peacefulness as possible. A time for wallowing while the wallowing was good, as already

native drums were banging out the news . . . I-R-O-N-B-I-R-D . . . I-R-O-N-B-I-R-D . . . over and over; soon the Crüe Two would be taking their leave, flying out as they'd flown in on the McGhee boneshaker. That much was clear, but the rest of the message, now that was a little more difficult to decipher; something to do with travel and something to do with a man of steel, no, no, a man of . . . *iron* . . . I-R-O-N-M-A-N. That was it.

With the drums still tapping out their vision of the future, Vince and Tommy bid fond farewell to this island retreat and soared into the sunset. Miami was their first scheduled stop and then a freezing Boston, Massachusetts, where they were due to meet up with colleagues and start rehearsals at Long View Farm, a secluded ten-bedroom house-farm-recording-rehearsal studio previously used by the Rolling Stones. Seems the Crüe had a show to do at the 9500-capacity Cumberland City Civic in Portland Maine, their first night as support act on a major US tour, and with January 10 1984 the date of the Portland gig, there wasn't much time to whip the music into shape. And the headline act? Ozzy Osbourne, of course, the old *iron man* himself.

Moral: native drummers may not have a deal with Sonor but their beat is true.

Vince spent New Year's Eve in the West Indies with Tommy just before the Ozzy Osbourne tour of the US.

Act Seven Mötleymania!

'The Ozzy tour was the turning point in Mötley Crüe's career. People were already curious but, up to that point, we were only selling to the real rock'n'roll maniacs' – Nikki Sixx

THIS WAS the first time. My initiation. Just prior to the release of the *Shout At The Devil* LP, I'd interviewed Nikki and Vince for *Kerrang!*, the three of us (plus chaperon Tom Zutuat) meeting up in the rather stilted surrounds of an LA hotel room. But it wasn't until Ozzy's '84 trek across the US that I got the chance to catch them live – in the flash, as it were.

I remember it well: January 20, the Providence Rhode Island Civic Center, ten days into the tour. I remember the rickety twin-prop plane that got me there in a state vaguely approaching one piece. I remember the ice and the snow and the mean, swirling wind, and I remember that it wasn't actually the Crüe I'd travelled out to see. No, top spot on my list was held by Ozzy Osbourne, the ol' ghoul-keeper himself, back to spread his own particular brand of outrage across the Great American Heartland. *He* was the reason I'd quit home and hearth this time around, but then Mötley Crüe aren't exactly the sort of band you can easily ignore. When they're there you know it, and when you know it you don't forget . . .

To East Coast audiences, this was all new and exciting, a trifle weird perhaps but with definite overtones of wonderful. They'd seen the pictures, they'd heard the stories, now was the time to sweep caution aside and grab a personal piece of the action. To the good folk of such places as Glens Falls and Binghampton NY State, the Crüe were an unknown quantity, but with local stores suddenly shifting all stocks of hairspray and dye (Nice'N'Easy as first choice, of course) and with ancient Kiss make-up kits rooted out from deepest, darkest cupboards for the first time in many (black) moons, the younger elements at least were more than willing to learn.

At the Providence show and the next night (January 21) at a near sold-out Boston Gardens, as many of the 10,000 or so in attendance had the Mötley logo stretched across

heaving chests as that of the headline head-snapper, and most unofficial merchandise bore the legend of both. For the first third of the tour, apart from gigs at The Stabler Arena, Bethlehem Pennysylvania, and Madison Square Garden, New York, the Ozzy/Crüe package was preceded by a third band on the bill – UK outfit Waysted. Featuring ex-UFO bassist/carouser Pete Way, a one-time (albeit brief) member of Ozzy's band and a man with the unique distinction of having introduced former Kiss guitarist Ace Frehley to the joys of Carlesberg Special Brew lager, they certainly pulled a good few of the crowd onto their side of the fence, but it was clearly the filling-in-the-sandwich boyzz who were making the most conversions.

Delivering with true missionary zeal, they successfully immersed those present in a tidal wave of tack, their set (as I wrote of the Providence show) proving a 'heady/hedonistic concoction of gross-out raps, crowd-pleasing antics and lustful locomotive rock'n'roll, dead-legged guitarist Mick Mars . . . providing the basis for a sound heavy on spit and light on polish' (*Kerrang!* issue 64 March 22-April 4). Perched atop the mixing desk, peering through a forest of outstretched hands, my pupils

dilated, my nostrils flared and my jaw loosened at the hinges as the band ran through a selection of songs from their two LPs. Simply, it was hard to imagine this pulverising party-on-legs ever squeezing its well-rouged pout between the glistening walls of a lowly LA club; this was Coliseum Rock of the meanest kind – inflammatory, wild'n'wanton anthems designed to fly straight across the parental brow and lance the soul of the unprotected offspring. After all, James Dean and Marilyn Monroe were hits with kids rather than parents, and if it's good enough for them . . .

Exploding like uncorked lava, the Crüe (as they say) were moving air. With the crash of every chord a new heart was captured, and any still undecided and of the female persuasion could always be converted *after* the show – which may explain why certain members of Ozzy's crew seemed to spend more time on the Mötley tour bus than their own, and why Ozzy guitarist Jake E. Lee (rumoured to be joining the Crüe at one point) passed most of his hours on the road behind a large wet grin! With MC there's always plenty to go round. Says Nikki:

'We get paid in flesh 'cos our audiences are sluts, whores each

(Left-Right) Jake E. Lee, Tommy and Bob Paisley (bang! bang!).

and every one, male and female. All
they want out of life is to get fucked,
and I love it, I think it's great!'

THE FIRST leg of the Ozzy tour
ran for forty three dates (January
10-March 24), ending with a sold-out
show at the 900-capacity Portland
Coliseum, Oregon, in the course of
which trek the band received gold
and platinum awards for sales of the
Shout . . . album in the US – the
former pressed into their hands at
the Limelight nightclub, Manhattan,
on January 29 and the latter
(signifying one million copies sold)
at the Madison Square Garden show
the day after – and the suspension of
their tour bus received more than a
thorough testing.

As for Ozzy, well, he was in fine
form, constantly burrowing deep
into Tommy's hair to reveal a pair of
pristine, Spock-like flaps and
explaining to the four that when it
came to matters of a crude or
excessive nature they were merely
pretenders to his well-appointed
throne. Fighting talk, I'd say, and
certainly words the Mötley men
weren't prepared to swallow easily;
after all, on the West Coast at least,
there were none more skilled in the
execution of the gross act or the
imaginative insult. These boys had
'studied' long and hard to get some
of those more difficult under-the-
table moves down pat, emerging as
gurus for a generation intent on
sliding a drawing pin under the
descending nether quarters of
polite society. They were good,
professional partyers, and once
battle had been joined, Ozzy had to
pull out all available stops to keep
his crown in place . . .

'He really *is* a madman, though,'
says Nikki, clearly meaning the
observation as a compliment. 'In this
one place, we were sitting around
and he's pissing all over the pool.
Then he gets down and laps it up,
and after that he starts snorting ants!'

'So we get this competition
underway – *who* can be more
extreme. He says "top this!" and
when we get into his dressing room
he's in drag; he went on-stage in a
garter belt, fishnets, a black lace
dress and a white wig. And this was
in Jacksonville, Florida (The
Coliseum). We were both banned
from the city for life; it'll take a court
order to get us back on-stage there!'

All a matter of double standards,
really. I mean, Pat Benatar often goes
out on the boards dressed as a
woman and she's never been
banned from anywhere. And what

about Boy George?! When Ozzy
does it, though, it's a different
story . . . As for Crue – well, they
incurred the wrath of local
wheelchair-bound, gout-ridden
authorities both for turning the air a
bright shade of blue with consistent
on-stage cussing and for admitting
to believing in the Devil on national
TV. The fact that the Pope would
have said exactly the same thing
didn't seem to matter; believing was
instantly taken to mean
'worshipping' and that was that,
leaving the band to ponder whether
they or Ozzy had emerged with the
sillier tag. Was it better or worse to
be judged a rocky horror than a
sweet transvestite – a Satanic sheep
or a limp-wristed lamb? Who
knows? But the MC liking for the
pentagram was in no way blunted by
this particular scenario, and quite
right too . . .

'I did some research at one time
and I came across things like the
swastika and the pentagram which
were ancient symbols. They really
had no evil meaning at all,' Nikki told
Andy Secher in *Hit Parader*
magazine (August '84). 'We kind of
liked the way the pentagram
looked, so we started using it as a
logo for the band. It was something
that was easily recognisable, and
that was the real reason we used it.

Believe me, it doesn't mean that we
give a fuck about the Devil. The only
things I care about are rock'n'roll,
chicks, and my bottle of Jack
Daniels. Who the hell would care
about the Devil when you can have
things like that?'

But what about all the religious
protesters who'd turned out on the
Ozzy/Crüe tour, persisted Secher, a
question that connected with Nikki
somewhere around the funny
bone . . .

'What are those clowns all about
anyhow?' he asked. 'Don't they know
that they're just attracting more
attention to us, and making us more
famous than ever? They're defeating
the whole purpose of what they're
trying to do. It's the most insane
thing I've ever seen. Ozzy was great
about it. He'd been through it all
before, and he had this 'fuck 'em all'
attitude. He just laughed at them. All
those protesters didn't even realise
that the joke was on them. We were
selling out all these arenas, and in
the meantime they were standing
out in the snow with their signs,
freezing their asses off.'

At the previously mentioned
Portland show, however, Mötley
Crüe (the 'court jesters', the 'clowns')
found that it was certainly possible
to look pretty damn silly *inside* an
arena as well. It was the group's last

date with Ozzy – for the moment at least – and the Mad Diarist was determined not to let the occasion pass without a hug, a handshake and a very special send-off; something to remember him by.

Again Andy Secher lent a sympathetic ear . . .

'All day long everytime I saw Ozzy he had this evil glint in his eye – something crazy was up for that night,' Nikki told him in *Hit Parader* (November '84). 'When we got on-stage we noticed two extra lighting guys up in the rafters, and they had these huge sacks of flour. As soon as we started playing, they started dropping flour on us. They did that for the full forty minutes we were on-stage. By the time we finished we looked like the Pillsbury Doughboys. Then when we started walking off-stage, Ozzy and his band started hitting us with custard pies – it was some mess, but it was a lot of fun.'

And there was more to come. *Much* more. I mean, no way were the

Crüe going to accept their fate like men. This was rock'n'roll, right? You didn't *have* to grow up, so with smirking schoolboy glee 'Operation Knobswing' was duly selected from their repertoire of wind-ups. Nikki explained:

'(Ozzy) has these crew members who dress like monks and walk on-stage during the set. We borrowed the monk outfits and walked on-stage with the robes on. The trick was we were naked underneath and we kept flashing the band as we walked across the stage. Then we went back to our dressing room, picked up all the food we could carry and went back to the stage. We must have pelted them with fifty pounds of potato salad while they were playing. Ozzy's about the coolest person you'll ever meet – nothing seems to rattle him – but I think he forgot the words to a few songs that night!'

I don't doubt it.

DEVIL-WORSHIPPING and dong-flashing aside, the Ozzy dates, in the words of Tommy, 'really whipped the group into shape'. They were able to make use of a few effects though nothing too spectacular, and so had to rely on purely musical abilities to pull them through, proving to everyone (including themselves) that, yes, they could play well *and* consistently. It was also around the beginning of this tour that Nikki made the revolutionary decision to move away from platform boots and into something a little more comfortable (not to mention contemporary).

The original idea behind the high-rise heels had been to make the band as a whole look more imposing, intimidating if you like, and with Nikki virtually born and bred in stilettos the transition to the classic simplicity of the baseball boot wasn't easy to come to terms with. After years of tottering around, hair brushing constantly against rafters and beams, it was tough to come back down to earth – too tough for Mick, in fact, who decided to remain as one with his platforms a little while longer, though Vince and Tommy both pitched in with the bassist in his drive towards more sensible, stylised footwear. Truly the end of an era(sob), yet just to keep Crüe fans (literally) on their toes Nikki would now appear to have shifted into natty Cuban heeled affairs, a real up and down ride that seems unlikely to stop until he's sampled the delights of the customised clog and the stack-heeled Wellington boot. We shall see . . .

Left: clipping from *BAM* magazine (December 26, 1982). Right: Saxon's Biff Byford, Vince and Stephen Pearcy from Ratt.

SURE OF FOOT and steady of nerve, the band embarked on a second series of major headline shows (US only) in April and May of '84 – 14 dates in all, taking in California, Colorado, Texas, Kansas, Missouri, Ohio, Michigan, Illinois and Indiana, with two UK outfits filling the support slots. Barnsley boys Saxon played on all the dates bar one (The civic, San José, Nikki's hometown, on April 26) and Glasgow mob Heavy Pettin on four. By American standards, the gigs were fairly small, ranging between the 2950-capacity Music Hall in Cleveland, Ohio, and the 8500-capacity Roberts Stadium in Evansville, Indiana, but most were pretty packed and several sold out, including the 6000-seat Civic Auditorium in Bakersfield, California. At The Fox Theatre in Detroit (May 8) the concussion of the group's music brought part of the ceiling down, while in Chicago (The Aragon Ballroom May 11) a crazed fan grabbed Nikki's bass and busted off the head, causing Nikki to bust *his* head in return. 'Hey, it was my favourite guitar!' he says . . .

The Crüe's guiding star was clearly burning bright, though on May 15 they broke off from their own tour to complete another ten shows with Ozzy (having just got the flour out of their hair from the last one!), a minitrek encompassing two festival appearances in Kalamazoo, Michigan (Timber Ridge Ski Lodge), and Des Moines, Iowa

Brothers In Arms: at one time Ratt guitarist Robbin 'King' Crosby and the Motley bassist used to share an apartment in LA.

(Fairgrounds), the former proving very eventful indeed with Triumph, Night Ranger, Ratt, Quiet Riot and Accept also featuring on the bill and Ozzy taking a swing at Rioteer Rudy Sarzo in a bar. It was the final flare-up in a disagreement that had been smouldering for quite some time, though it wasn't really the mild-mannered Sarzo (now split from QR) who Ozzy was after; he just happened to be in the wrong place at the wrong time.

No, the man he actually wanted to get his hands on was Quiet Riot vocalist and all-round mouth Kevin Dubrow, a veteran of the LA scene who'd been saying less than complementary things about him – and Mötley Crüe – in the US press ('He said that we suck, that we're posers and that we'd never sell a record'-Nikki). But with Mr Dubrow arriving in the company of four bodyguards it was the unprotected

and innocent Sarzo who ended up on the deck. A shame, though the 52,000 or so who turned up for the American Rock Festival could have had no idea that more action was going down *behind* the stage than on it . . . or could they? One eyewitness source is prepared to swear long and hard that at a certain point the various members of Mötley Crüe and Quiet Riot had to be led away from a heated word war because the crowd out front could no longer hear the band on-stage, but the report is unconfirmed. Sounds feasible, mind . . .

Certainly, the two bands continued to go for each other's throats in the press, though following a *Kerrang!* interview with Nikki Sixx (issue 73, July 26-August 8 1984), in the course of which the receding DuBrow hairline came in for a good deal of abuse – 'I guess his head's got so big that it's growing

through his hair!' – some kind of truce was apparently struck, with Kevin making the first conciliatory call. The feud, for the moment at least, was on ice . . .

ANYONE FOLLOWING the Mötley Crüe/Quiet Riot furore blow by bitter blow might well have come to the understandable conclusion that none of the LA bands get on too well, which isn't actually the case. Sure, rivalry does exist, and one-time friends have been known to fall out, usually over a thoughtless word or two (sometimes more) in the press, but there's also a good deal of neighbourly concern – like between Mötley Crüe and Ratt, for example.

At one point, Nikki and Ratt guitarist Robbin Crosby used to share an apartment in the city and today, when touring or recording commitments don't impose, the two are often to be found tucking eagerly into a Mexican meal or a similarly spicy female at a favourite local haunt. I guess you could say they're best friends – Nikki addresses Robbin as 'King' and the latter reciprocates with 'Leader', and in earlier times both were to be found fighting back against the world in Hollywood street gang the Gladiators, also numbering Ratt vocalist Stephen Pearcy in its ranks – so it must have been particularly satisfying when, following the aforementioned festivals, Mötley Crüe embarked on thirteen headline shows with Ratt supporting on seven of them.

Starting with a sold-out gig at the 2800-capacity Landmark theatre in Syracuse, New York State, the tour took the Crüe on into Massachusetts, Pennsylvania and various Canadian cities – including Montreal (Verdon Arena) and Toronto (CNE Coliseum), two wall-to-wall shows – where they were supported either by local outfits or German heavy rockers Accept. In terms of sheer prestige though, it was probably MC's two sell-out appearances at Manhattan's Beacon Theatre that meant the most. A mere eighteen months earlier the future of the band had been very much in the balance (it had to be everything or nothing and no-one knew which), yet now here they were, riding around in limos and running the gauntlet of screaming fans.

On June 2 and 3, the days of the Beacon shows, almost every major Manhattan hotel had a small posse of girls hanging out in the lobby, some clutching flowers and gifts, most simply clutching at straws – except that is for the well-informed few who chose to deposit their ardour outside That Mayflower, a noted rock'n'roll guesthouse on Central Park West and Sixty-First Street. They'd done their homework, ten out of ten, their reward being a fleeting glimpse of blond or blue-black mane as, under the expert surveillance of tour manager Rich 'Fish' Fisher, the four celebrity Crüesters placed chins on chests and made a headlong burst for the shiny black sanctuary of the nearest available limo. The price of fame – or should that be infamy? Who cares! Whatever it was it was working a treat, even getting through to an initially reluctant label . . .

'Y'know,' says Nikki, 'it's not a good feeling when you walk down the hallway of your record company and everybody comes out and says "hi", and you're thinking, wait a minute, wasn't it just seven months ago that the secretaries screamed, ran into the offices and locked the doors when we walked past? And we get off on that. We'll always be rebels . . .'

The Crüe were being given the full red carpet treatment by the folk in the big seats at Elektra, but as far as they were concerned there was no good reason why they shouldn't use it to wipe muddy feet. After all, with well over a million copies of the *Shout At The Devil* LP already sold in the States at nine bucks a throw (the figure is now about 2.5 million/3 million worldwide and rising), *they'd* probably paid for the carpet; and if they felt in need of a little salty refreshment they saw no good reason not to lick on hungry lips and bite down deep into somebody's arm. Why muck around, y'know?! Playful pecks? No way! when Nikki and co set their incisors to work they seldom relax until blood has been smelt and their victims sent packing for a course of human bite injections – a sensible move as any female underwear thrown onto the stage tends to pass through Nikki's mouth before being suspended from a convenient backline 'spike'. The taste and aroma appeal to him, it seems, particularly if the garment in question has been, shall we say, soiled. That's the trouble with Mötley Crüe, you never know where they've been . . .

'If people travel with us on the road, we just bite the fuck out of 'em!' warns Nikki, who looks capable of biting off quite a lot and chewing it as well. 'It's fun . . . unless you've been bitten, I guess.'

And do they flex their molars on each other? Of course they do!

'We go for each other regular,' adds the bas(e)ist, 'Tommy and I bite each other all the time. It's crazy!'

Footnote one: human bites are worse than an animal's because of the bacteria in the saliva and require a tetanus shot if the skin gets broken; everyone in the Mötley Crüe camp knows this – they *have* to.

Footnote two: the band will only bite people they like.

THE CRÜE, it seems, could get away with almost anything; if they weren't biting people (from management through to waitresses) then they were *tying them up* and biting them (the fate of an unfortunate video jockey). And when they weren't giving vent to that particular whim, they were probably scrawling suggestive graffiti on the nearest stationary object and/or person. As already mentioned, Tommy is by far the most adventurous on this front, cultural instincts dating back to ancient Ionic civilisation clearly guiding his hand. The uninhibited sweep of the pen,

For those about to rock: Motley fans salute their heroes.

Nikki makes his mark at Private Eye's video club, Manhattan.

the inherent feel for composition and colour, the boy is unquestionably a natural, though like all great innovators shamefully misunderstood.

What critics have pilloried as offensive and obscene, Tommy merely sees as earthy self-expression, better out than in, with anatomical studies plainly a speciality. Some, head to one side, staring one-eyed over upright thumb, have likened his work in this field to a 'crystallised banana', others a 'cucumber *en repose*', and others . . . well, we won't go into that; suffice it to say, that by the time the Crüe took their second bite of the Big Apple in June '84 they were pretty damn cocky with *everything* on the rise. Clearly, this was their time, their moment of conquest, though an ill-arranged record signing session at Private Eyes video club on Twenty-first Street added just a hint of droop to previously rampant parts. On this occasion, the earth did not move . . .

The original idea had been for the band to make an in-store apperance at the massive Manhattan branch of Tower Records, but many feared that such a brazen showing might simply be too much for young hearts

and minds to safely absorb. Hence the switch to somewhere altogether more discreet, with advance publicity kept to a minimum. Well, that was the theory and the practice proved devastatingly effective, reducing a potential Crüe-crazed mob, all mouth and short skirt, to a heavily subdued, rather pathetic trickle.

Still, at least those who picked up on the event, by accident or design, got the rare opportunity to do the rounds more than once, a chance to get *both* knees (or whatever!) consummately carboned and take a good long look at the three Mötley videos, looped up and bursting out of every available screen. Did I say three? Actually, there are *five*, though the band's first tentative steps into the brave new video age (*'Take Me To The Top'/'Public Enemy 1'*) have long been deemed unfit for viewing by anyone other than immediate group members; to lapse briefly into technical film jargon, they are what the likes of Orson Welles and Steven Spielberg would probably describe as 'crap', and pretty low-budget 'crap' at that, so a treble bill it was with Nikki and co taking up customary positions in the dusky back row.

Passed by the censor then were; 1) *Live Wire*, a 700-dollar 'live' extravaganza, featuring leading man Rhett Sixx with heart and boots ablaze; 2) *Looks That Kill*, a 50,000-dollar fantasy epic lacking neither for women nor humour, and 3) *Too Young To Fall In Love*, the follow-up directed by Martin Kahan at a cost of 75,000 dollars. Shot using six sets and fifteen actors in a cold, damp, abandoned subway tunnel under a warehouse on Twelfth Avenue, NY, it took some forty eight hours to get down on film (expensive 35mm), during which time Crüe publicist Bryn Bridenthal had to keep a very close eye on the thirteen year old girl chosen to portray the subject of the song.

My responsibility as 'mom' is to make sure that the boys don't manhandle their co-star!' she told *Faces Rocks* magazine (August '84) in exasperated tones, though the girl's parents sensibly remained on the set for every moment of the shooting.

'Her dad told me that he went down to the record store to pick up a Mötley Crüe record to see what it was all about, and when he opened it up, he threw it up in the air in shock and amazement, he was horrified!'

Still, the video was excellent, highly entertaining stuff (if a little derivative of Kiss' *All Hell's Breakin' Loose* effort, also directed by Kahan), with Nikki and Tommy going on to accept cameo roles as policemen in Ratt's *Back For More* promo and the Crüe also having a presence in the latter's *You Think You're Tough* clip. Clearly, video had emerged as an important new outlet for the Mötley Möguls, whose washout appearance at Private Eyes must have brought back early career memories of an equally unspectacular signing session in Grass Valley, the four of them sticking out farther than Tommy's ears or Vince's hair after prolonged Pantene (a favourite hair-spray) abuse. They'd played a couple of shows there hoping to lay a groundswell of support, but despite an upwind position at the local record store it soon became clear, painfully so, that no-one wanted them to sign anything – not record, not T-shirt, not torso, not *nothing*! In fact, they were barely noticed, unusual for them, though by the time of the New York debacle (a genuine exception) a Mötley Crüe PA had become less of a sedate scribbling scenario than an explosive rough'n'tumble; the chance to pin a kiss to a front cover face (I'm talkin' girls here, of course) or better still grab a hunk of hair and refuse to let go.

Clearly, these are not places for the weak of knee or the frail of bladder. Indeed, upon departing such an event the band are under strict instructions to perform a quick bodily check, a way of ensuring that nothing vital – an arm, a leg, or worse(!) – has been left behind, though sometimes it can be a close run thing. *Damn* close. An in-store appearance in West Covina California, for example, attracted around 3000 riotous fans, while in May '84, in Tampa Florida on the Ozzy tour, the four had to be taken away to safety in a helicopter! Once in Seattle and a couple of times in Texas (they always have to go one better there!) rampant Crüe supporters, not content with just hanging onto the band's limo, decided to try and turn it over – anything to stop their heroes escaping into the sunset.

Frankly, it's not unusual for the 'heroes' in question to have items of clothing ripped from their very person, sometimes in the course of a PA and sometimes *after* it! On one memorable occasion, they leapt blindly into the back of a van

preparing to be whisked away to their hotel, only to discover two girls already waiting for them inside, stripped to the skin and clutching only the remains of the ignition system. A *fait accompli*. What could they do but applaud such ingenuity and resign themselves to their fate? Yeah, it's tough at the top and, in this sense at least, no-one's had it tougher than Mötley Crüe . . . STORIES OF Nikki tying girls to tree trunks and 'filling them up' with bottles have become legendary in metal circles, and, as *Hit Parader* Editor-In-Chief John Shelton Ivany told men's magazine *Hustler* (April '85), 'the kids marvel at incidents like this. In fact, girls have written to us asking "why didn't Nikki stick that bottle in me?" '

Well, be fair, the guy has only got one pair of hands y'know, it probably just *seems* like more. As he explained to Dennis Hunt in *Calendar* (Sunday November 13 1983) 'women are one of our primary motivations . . . We have a collection of polaroid shots of groupies we've met on the road. We like to pick up a bunch of girls in one town and take 'em on the tour bus to the next town . . . (our manager) tells us only to pick up rich groupies. Those are usually the fat ones . . . We've found the fat ones are really the best – they're willing to do anything.'

The only trouble is, you don't score as many points for a 'fattie'. The system, according to Vince, works like this: 'ten points for a centrefold type chick, one point for a good-looking chick and five de-merit points for an ugly one', with Tommy apparently lagging well behind, but game nonetheless. Of course, he may still come with a late, uh, spurt, though it can be rather difficult to bump up your total when, as Nikki explained to the ever-receptive Secher (*Hit Parader* November '84), 'we're not the type of band that's gonna get Farrah Fawcett backstage after the show. We get the chicks who just love to have fun. They don't have any pretense about them – they know what they want, and they know that we'll give them more than they can handle. In a way, it's a shame Farrah doesn't come to our shows, because after a gig I'm sure we could show her the time of her life.'

Yeah, I reckon she'd get through without a PSP pass (standing for 'Pre-Show Pussy' and indicating to the band that the bearer has already 'entertained' the road crew in order to get the pass and hence best left untouched), probably finding herself at the receiving end of some

favourite Crüe moves. In the August '84 issue of *Hit Parader* Vince spelt out to Secher exactly what that can mean – 'the other day we had this one chick in the van and she was hanging over the seat naked. She was doing Nikki on one side, and we were shoving a beer bottle in her on the other side of the seat' – an article that eventually found its way to the NFD (National Federation of Decency) after a mother discovered her thirteen year old son reading the mag. Clearly, she was shocked that these graphic goings-on could be reported in a publication openly on sale at Wal-Mart, K-Mart and the like alongside such titles as *Field and Stream*, yet the fact remains that many Crüe fans are very young and, it must be said, anything but innocent – probably able to teach their parents a trick or two on the carnal cavorting front.

Disagree if you will, but that was certainly the conclusion reached by San Antonio radio station KISS-FM following a promotion involving the band. The idea was this: that listeners, male or female, should send in their answers to a simple question and the ones judged the best would receive free tickets to an upcoming Mötley Crüe show and maybe even get taken backstage to meet the band.

The question: 'What would you do to meet the Crüe?'

The answers (reported by colomnist Bob Greene in the May '84 issue of *Esquire* magazine) left nothing to the imagination . . .

From a sixteen year old girl:
'What I would do to see Mötley Crüe. First, I would tie you up, spread-eagle and naked, with leather straps. Then I'd shave all the hair off your chest, and if I should nick you, I'll suck up all the blood as it slowly trickles down your body. Next I'll cover your body with motion lotion to get things really heated up. When it gets *too* hot, I'll cover your body in crushed ice and lay on top of you to melt it down and cool you off.'

'Then I'll do things to your body with my tongue that you never thought humanly possible. Then when you are screaming for mercy and begging for more, telling me how you want it all, I'll slam the spiked heel of my right leather boot into your navel, call you a very naughty boy, and laugh as I slowly walk away, telling you I'm just not that kind of girl.'

From a thirteen year old girl:
'I'd do *it* with the Crüe 'till black and blue is all you can see.'

From a fifteen year old girl:
'I'm really a big fan of Mötley

Tommy and 'friend' getting their act together for *Oui* magazine.

Crüe's and I would do anything to meet them . . . I love 'em all. I would even get fucked by the ugliest, fattest, most disgusting guy in the world to meet them . . .'

From a thirteen year old girl:
'I'd leave my tits to Mötley Crüe.'

From a fourteen year old boy:
'I would give them my mother, who is very beautiful. She has red hair and brown eyes. She loves heavy metal and especially Mötley Crüe. My mother definitely has *the looks that kill*.'

No doubt intrigued by this last response, Greene decided to contact the boy's thirty-four year old mother and check things out for himself. Did she mind? Apparently not . . .

'Billy and I have a good mother-and-son relationship,' she responded. 'He's crazy about me and I'm crazy about him. When Billy said that he had offered me to the band, I said "Oh, Billy". But I really do like them, and I would like to help Billy win the contest.'

The lure of rock'n'roll. Wherever the Crüe go, girls are sure to follow.

It's both a cross they have to bear and the reason why they continue to look forward to the rest of the day (what's left of it, anyway) when they throw back the sheets and hit the shower after a hard night on the town. Says Nikki, an incorrigible (female) flesh-eater who lived with ex-Runaways guitarist Lita Ford for a year (she introduced herself to the bassist by offering him half a quaalude – on her tongue!), 'I didn't get in a band 'cos I wanted a Ferrari; I got in a band 'cos I wanted to get laid.'

He's succeeded.

Act Eight
Continental Capers-
The Second Front

'Castle Donington? . . . very few bottles!' – Doc McGhee.

IN EUROPE, and particularly the UK, everything's just that little bit different. For a start, the whole media set-up means that young girls are more likely to be into pop than rock music, which is fine if you happen to be Duran Duran or Spandau Ballet but not so good if you're squarely synched in with the HM fraternity. For the latter, long walks and cold showers are often the only option, which may well be the reason, or part of it at least, why US bands tend not to spend too much time in the UK. I mean, we all know Detroit-born guitar-showman Ted Nugent's views on the English Rose, don't we? ('You seen the women in London lately?! One day is all we'll need to service everything! You know, the last time I played Hammersmith Odeon I looked out there in the front row and I thought the *pig* season had opened!!') Well, we do now, and I can recall having many open-heart discussions with young Jake E. Lee about matters not too far removed.

'Tell me, how do people in Britain ever get themselves laid?' he'd ask in earnest as we fought our way into yet another crowded pub.

'I don't know,' I'd reply, removing an elbow from my ear, 'but one thing's for sure, if it never happened it would be a hell of a lot easier to get a drink!'

At the Castle Donington Festival, Mötley Crüe's first ever UK show in the hot, hot Summer of '84, Nikki too started feeling a touch low of spirit, kicking the turf backstage with the air of someone who'd found a dollar and lost a friend.

'Are my eyes red?' he enquired, momentarily removing the ever-present shades, and I had to admit

Nikki at the Castle Donington festival, August 18, 1984.

that they were . . . a little. Unable to locate any suitably compliant females, he'd clearly been seeking solace from that great guru of our times, the Very Reverend Jack D. The man needed help.

'Look!' I shouted, pointing out a sweet young thing, all black stockings and come-on smile, but like so many good 'uns before him he'd clearly lost hope. A shame, though Tommy I'm glad to say was still his old self, lusty, lewd and completely legless – a man who, following a Crüe photo session with *Oui* magazine (November '82), went AWOL in the company of one of the female models and wasn't seen again for three whole days!

'Hey there,' he slurred, draping an arm around my shoulder, 'if my balls were hanging down by your chin, where would my cock be?!'

Ummm . . . well I thought I knew the answer and judging from the wide open grin on his face (not to mention everyone else's within a five-mile radius – this guy is *loud*!) it was evident I was right.

64,000 dollars, pleeze!

SCHEDULED FOR Saturday August 18, the Donington show was an important one for Mötley Crüe, no doubt about that, and they certainly weren't taking it lightly – whatever the previous paragraphs might lead you to believe. They finished their third US headline tour on June 15 1984, playing to a crowd of almost 8000 at The Civic Center in Springfield, Massachusetts, then set their sights on Europe; a dream made real at last. Nikki as ever was confident ('We *will* leave an impression!' he told me a couple of months earlier in a New York hotel room strewn with clothes, sunglasses and the odd leather whip), but with Accept, Y&T, Gary Moore, Ozzy, Van Halen and AC/DC also on the bill, and all proven acts in these parts, the task of launching the number one outdoor event in the UK rock calendar was inevitably going to fall on the Crüe. Had Doc and Doug combined to kick up a big enough fuss they could probably have got the band promoted above Accept, but what the hell! If they had to do things the hard way, from the bottom up, then so be it, though many felt the decision to send their boys into battle in this lowly slot an act of rank foolishness tantamount to suicide.

First group on, eh? No lights, of course, and no access to the video screen, too early in the day for that squire, and no stage set to speak of beyond basic backline, *that* you have to expect. And then there's the

sound; if you're lucky and it doesn't rain and the wind blows in the right direction, those at the back might *just* be able to make out what you're playing, but with no use of the delay towers (for the main act only, you understand) it's all a bit of a risk.

Problems, problems, problems. To stake your reputation on a performance at a gig like this clearly requires considerable raw nerve and a great deal of guts. A safer bet would have been for the Crüe to headline their own show prior to the Donington appearance, a night at the celebrated Hammersmith Odeon perhaps, giving them a chance to impress on their own terms before jumping head-first into the festival lottery. But then that simply wasn't (and isn't) the Mötley method. All or nothing, remember? And besides, the four had no intention at all of letting anyone down – least of all themselves . . .

When they hit the stage at twelve noon, a full thirty minutes before their publicised appearance time, they were psyched up to wreak maximum havoc, removing the mid-paced 'Shout At The Devil' from the front of the set and hitting hard an' fast with 'Bastard', Allan Coffman's ears no doubt glowing yet again. *Kerrang!* journalist Derek Oliver, stationed out front amidst the 60,000-plus crowd, was rocked back on his heels, gleefully proclaiming that the Crüe's success 'hasn't been built on image alone. The band rip out *real* metal thunder, brighter and heavier than any other LA act you care to mention. The likes of Quiet Riot are simply laughable in comparison.'

Final act of silliness from the *Oui* session (November 1983).

'Rampaging through a selection of their best cuts, the Crüe turned initial indifference to positive appreciation. By the time they reached 'Ten Seconds To Love' the crowd were eating out of their hands and victory had undeniably been secured . . .' (issue 76 September 6–19 1984).

In the past, the opening position at Donington has generally been considered something of a booby prize, the graveyard spot, the role of the band being apparently to draw the fire of the heavily armed front rows (missiles, mud, whatever) in order to make things safer for the really big egos twitching nervously in the wings. Touch, More, Anvil, Diamond Head – over its celebrated history the festival has proved more of a U-bend than a turning point for those first into the fray, though hopefully Mötley Crüe have now broken that jinx . . . for good.

'Oh, we'd heard all the horror stories,' says Vince, 'that we were gonna get bombarded with bottles, cans and rocks, *everything* y'know. But when we finally came to do it, sure we had a couple of things thrown at us, but we weren't pelted. I mean, I saw stuff being thrown at Van Halen and AC/DC too.'

It's true that Mötley Crüe were a good deal weightier in terms of reputation than others who'd occupied the 'Aunt Sally' spot, but had they proved little more than arch LA hypesters, all flash and no bang, then I doubt vey much if that would have saved them. Nossir!

On the day, it was attitude and musical ability, no more no less, that pulled them through unscathed, the four barely noticing the absence of their two semi-trailers (250,000 dollars-worth of gear, sets and props). To be totally accurate, a portion of calf's liver *did* land somewhere on-stage, closely followed by a cow's eye, but the Crüe weren't about to let that bother them, showing a resilience and strength of purpose that made a deep, lasting impression on rock fan and broadcaster Jonathan King. So inspired was the man that he not only wrote nice things about the band in the music press, freely dropping words such as 'courage' and 'respect', but he also allowed them to have their photo taken with him, a rare honour indeed . . .

Show-time over, the four festival anchörmen exploded out of the backstage area, all sloppy grins and boozy breath, a mobile party animal determined to leave both mark and scent on all uncovered flesh – being an almost unbearably hot day there was certainly no shortage of that, which was good news for Tommy's crayon and Nikki's teeth but not such glad tidings for Mick's (ever so) pale face. Finished as always in matt black, he did all he could to keep in the shade, leaving Nikki to take care of the energetic stuff like hoisting members of other groups for the benefit of roving lensmen and retiring to the group's backstage trailer to hurl vodka bottles out of the window. Sounds a mite dangerous to me, though earlier out front he'd decided to hurl around his Hamer bass, tossing it into the crowd 'as a gift' . . . and performing an instant, unrehearsed lobotomy on the 'lucky' recipient in the third row! That's the thing about Mötley Crüe; when Nikki says 'we play blood'n'guts rock'n'roll – we bleed for the audience', he sometimes expects the audience to bleed back.

Question: should all hardened Crüe fans know their blood type:

Answer: only if they're sensible. THIS, HOWEVER, was just the start of the band's European campaign. One week later (August 25) they were breaking the ice with Swedish crowds in Stockholm, opening band yet again on a festival bill that paralleled the Donington line-up (with a single exception; out went Y&T and in came Dio, the Anglo-American brainchild of one-time Rainbow/Black Sabbath vocalist Ronnie James Dio), the entire package rumbling on from one country to the next, heaving on the brake at selected sites in Winterthur

(August 31), Karlsruhe (September 1) – a German football stadium housing a vociferous number of American GIs – Nurnburg(2), Nettuno(5) and Torino(7). Seven major shows inside a three week period, certainly a cause for celebration, and it was indeed with cups running over that Tommy, Mick and Vince bid their farewells and returned to LA. Nikki stayed on for a while, spending a few relaxing days in '*belle* Paris' with the press hanging on his every word, then flew back to join his colleagues in the studio.

With their all-important third album very much in mind, the band proceeded to lay down demos of three new songs – 'Tonight (We Need A Lover)', described by Nikki as 'kinda 'Looks That Kill' meets Judas Priest', 'Save Our Souls' and 'Raise Your Hands To Rock', the title of the latter coming direct from the lips of Carmine Appice – the excellent (if somewhat nomadic) drummer currently guarding the beat with young LA outfit King Kobra. Carmine being Carmine, and that means lively with the mouth, 'Raise . . .' wasn't the only banner to trip off his silver-coated tongue. Let's see . . . there was 'Mad Dog Lover' . . . oh, and 'Bonecrusher Blues' – real subtle, candle-lit *soirée* stuff – though it was his first suggestion that Nikki liked best, an imagination-grabber of the best kind. He put down the phone, receiver still aglow, reached for the nearest guitar and a new number was born – *presto!* – the end result occupying track four side two of the *Theatre Of Pain* LP. 01' catalyst Carmine had done it again . . .

Pleased with the demos, the Crüe stuffed all important possessions into well-travelled totes and jetted off to London post haste; Iron Maiden had just completed a sold-out UK tour with Waysted in support and were poised to start a series of headline dates in Europe for which the Mötley boys had their name and number clearly pencilled in – twenty one shows, second-on-the-bill, across nine different countries. Vince's postcard-writing hand was already atwitch, though matters of this nature really can't be rushed. First, there was an *almighty* Iron Maiden party to attend at swanky, mirror-lined Legends nightclub, Old Burlington Street (October 12), in the course of which certain 'on the job' photos of Vince and Tommy were circulated quite freely and Xavier Russell was turned upside down and shaken by a (lack of drugs) crazed Nikki. And after

that . . . *almighty* hangovers . . . and after that . . . rehearsals at a 'little kids' gymnasium in London. 'There were all these eight to twelve year olds running around while we were in there playing and drinking whisky,' recalls Nikki with a smile. 'There were drawings all over the place, it was hilarious!'

Hilarious indeed, and quite a change from the venue they chose to rehearse in prior to their various festival appearances a couple of months earlier. That was a thirteenth century castle no less, recommended to them by those well known lords of the manor, AC/DC; a chance for the 'live for the present' Crüe to explore a piece of the past – even if it wasn't their own. But then how could it be? I mean, if they'd chosen to pay a call to the cultural centre of their *own* environment they'd probably have found

Nikki and Tommy (a rear view) at Donington.

themselves lodged in a Hollywood hamburger joint with nothing ancient to speak of outside of the fries! No, this was clearly the real thing, a genuine seat of medieval mayhem that Nikki wasted no time in capturing on his video camera, a permanent record of a journey back in time.

What more could they sensibly want? They had it all . . . a large upstairs room to rehearse in, a nearby country house to bed down in and the serene English countryside to relax in; the serene English countryside of Diss in Norfolk, to be precise, swiftly amended to 'No-fuck' when they discovered just what else they *did* sensibly want! 'A horse, a horse, my kingdom for a horse!' In a sudden frustrated flash the true meaning of those ancient, historical words became all too apparent; these were desperate times, demanding desperate action, the last (resort) waltz . . .

'There was *one* chick there but she was pregnant and fat at the same time and uglier than a beanstalk', recalls Nikki, wincing at the memory, 'and we ALL wanted her! There was hardly anybody else around, and the ones we did come across couldn't believe the way we looked. We had this jeep that we used to drive about in, one of those four-wheel drive things y'know, and as we'd be going down the street all these kids would come out of the nearby houses and shout "mum, look at the hippies!" They really thought we were HIPPIES,' he laughs, which makes you wonder just what the reaction might have been had Jerry Garcia and the Grateful Dead suddenly wafted past, smoke trailing wistfully from all available orifices.

'Hey, mum, look at the motley crew!' perhaps.

It's possible.

ON OCTOBER 15 1984 at the Sporthalle in Cologne, Germany, Mötley Crüe played the first of their twenty-plus European shows with Iron Maiden, going on to plant a flag in the name of US metal in a great many halles in a great many countries: the Rhein-Neckar-Halle in Heidelberg (October 17), the Carl-Diem-Halle in Wuerzberg(19), the Grugahalle in Essen(26) and so on, the tour finally coming to an end at (that's right) the Sporthalle St. Jakob in Basel, Switzerland on November 14. A well worthwhile outing that saw Nikki establish a firm and lasting friendship with Maiden vocalist Bruce Dickinson (the latter, an expert fencer, is currently

threatening to give him some lessons) and the band itself establish enough of a foothold to ensure that when they next return to Europe it'll certainly be in a headline capacity.

The trek enabled them to lay the necessary groundwork, though it wasn't all plain sailing with the 'culture shock' factor eventually taking its toll. Vince, who hadn't travelled on the continent before, found it all very edifying for a couple of weeks and after that, well . . . word has it that at a given hour of the day, *every* day, he'd turn both body and mind towards his Redondo Beach home and say a silent prayer, requesting God to save the souls of nearest'n'dearest and, if that was too much trouble, at least save him a seat at the Rainbow. A nice dark one in the corner. He was homesick . . .

'It was fun seeing different places like Venice, y'know, but eventually I thought, get me back to the States! Trying to talk to people in Europe was difficult (strange, I thought 'double chilli cheeseburger' was a universal phrase!) and figuring out all the different currencies wasn't easy either. Hey, I just like to watch TV and eat my junk food . . .'

As for Mr Mars, it seems he wasn't too keen on Holland, finding the Dutch media a touch on the bite-your-head-off side. 'I don't think they like us very much there,' is his only comment, and Nikki too found the people a little, shall we say, *different.*

'The kids were just fucked up out of their brains,' he laughs, though the Swedish crowds proved a touch more in control – if still betraying a certain wild look about the eyes – and the Germans, inevitably I suppose, came out top in the chanting stakes. *All* the different countries, however, were familiar with the songs, needing little encouragement to join in come chorus time, which put the band in a confident frame of mind for their final show before heading off home to the beckoning bosom of LA. It was an important one: a headline appearance at the 2800-capacity Dominion Theatre in the heart of London's West End on November 19. A chance for the Crüe to take the repect they'd earned from their Castle Donington outing and *double* it.

That had been a case of delivering on bare boards with the sun (nature's permanent follow-spot) blazing merrily overhead; a short, sharp shock to an audience still blinking the sleep out of its eyes. But at the Dominion with Stratus,

Culture shock for the Crüe: Mick found the Dutch media a touch on the tough side . . .

featuring ex-Iron Maiden drummer Clive Burr, in support they had the chance to make an altogether deeper impression and one that was all their own. They were well played in after the Maiden tour, they had a sell-out crowd totally at their mercy and they had the spanking new 'Raise Your Hands To Rock' primed and positioned in the set. What could possibly go wrong? Well . . .

With the dry-ice machine exploding *before* the show, burning the back of drum technician Clyde 'the Spide' Duncan, and Vince taking a tumble over a monitor *during* the show, it soon became

. . . while Vince missed his junk food and late-night TV.

clear that the answer to that question was 'quite a lot really'. And that wasn't the end of it. To make matters worse and dampen spirits still further some of the FX didn't behave to order, keeping the four constantly on their toes, and they generally felt that the response of the crowd was more lukewarm than lavish, a few stops down on the 'clapometer' from what they'd come to expect. In fact, that *hadn't* been the case, with first

album material being particularly well received and *Kerrang!* korrespondent Laura Canyon hailing the band as 'True Masters of Rock Mayhem' (issue 83 December 13-26 1984), but used to adulatory American audiences and the comforting heat from a sea of hoisted lighters, they were difficult to console.

Later in the evening at Legends, Vince surrounded himself with a

selection of dazzling blondes (just to take his mind off things, you understand) and Mick refused to allow disappointment to dry out his throat . . .

'You know,' he said, slipping slowly but surely from seat to floor, 'when I get home everybody thinks I'm gonna clean myself out . . . but I'm not! I'm gonna get more rotted than *ever!!*'

Heads were down but resolve remained intact. Clearly, there was to be no surrender. No way.

Final Scenes

Because there would inevitably be a gap of over eighteen months between albums, it was decided to release – in November of '84 (US only) – a 12″ pic disc EP focusing heavily on the 'Helter Skelter' track, complete with giant 23″ x 46″ full colour poster and special insert. Despite the fact that it contained nothing new, the record has now sold not far short of 100,000 copies, indicating that the number of Crüe fanatics was still on the increase and boding well for the release of the third album

On June 21 1985 the third Mötley Crüe LP, *Theatre Of Pain*, was unleashed on an anticipating public (it came out three days later in the UK). Recorded at Pasha, Cherokee and Record Plant West Studios and mixed at Record Plant West by producer Tom Werman and engineer Duane Baron, the band had at one time toyed with the title 'Louder Than Hell', but concluding that it didn't quite have the necessary ring, that certain *je ne sais quoi,* it was eventually changed to 'Entertainment Or Death', a line on the 'Keep Your Eye On The Money' track and a banner clearly reflecting Nikki's cherished 'all or nothing' philosophy. Indeed, certain bad taste overtones really couldn't be denied and it seems likely that the title may now be held in reserve for the first Crüe live album, unscheduled at the moment yet in the back of minds nonetheless.

So *Theatre Of Pain* it was – almost the title of the *Shout At The Devil* LP, incidentally – with rising star Baron replacing Geoff Workman on the technical side. Seems the band weren't too happy with the sound of the *Shout . . .* album, feeling it rooted pretty much in the '70s when they had both feet (all eight of 'em, in fact!) firmly planted in the here and now – the '80s.

'Geoff took away the rawness and the edge,' explains Nikki, 'the fact that we're always on the brink of falling apart when we're playing', which is why a more contemporary set of ears was duly introduced. For Tommy it was very good news indeed, a dream come true no less . . .

'Y'know, I've always dug Duane's work, I think he's incredible. When I knew he was gonna work with us I went to his house and played him a tape of this Cheap Trick song on the 'Up The Creek' soundtrack; it was the title track of the movie, and I went "this is the kind of drum sound I want, I just wish I knew how it was done", to which he replied "I did that!" I opened up the cassette case and there it was – 'engineered by Duane Baron'. He worked on the whole soundtrack, in fact, and I'd never bothered to look. I just wanted to kiss him, I couldn't believe it!'

Whether or not he managed to restrain himself isn't known, and Duane – a happily married man – certainly isn't telling, but I suspect it was a close run thing. Tommy was in excitable form, no doubt about that, a condition heightened by the quality of the new material with its bluesy, soulful edge . . .

'It's just more groove-orientated,' he explained. 'A lot of the *Shout At The Devil* stuff was kinda 'meat'n'potatoes', but the new songs are real chunky and groovy. And the band itself has become much, much better after being on the road for so long. Nikki's bass playing has come along incredibly, though he doesn't claim to be the best musician in the world. He is a hell of a songwriter, though . . .'

With the exception of 'Smokin' In The Boys Room', a cover version of the old Brownsville Station song selected in favour of Mountain's 'Mississippi Queen' and featuring Vince on harmonica, Nikki is the brains behind all the lyrics on the *TOP* album and the bass'n'brains behind the bulk of the music too. The swaggering 'City Boys Blues', track one side one; 'Louder Than Hell', an early(ish) number that once held sway in the live set under the title 'Hotter Than Hell' (amended perhaps to avoid confusion with the Kiss song, 'Keep Your Eye On The Money') originally to do with record company wheeling'n' dealing but changed (on the advice of Robbin Crosby) to the less controversial subject of gambling; 'Home Sweet Home', a ballad boasting Tommy on piano and Mick on showcase guitar stunts – these are all Nikki's songs. A move away from the norm.

Side two, meanwhile, features 'Tonight (We Need A Lover)', the opening line of which was switched from '40,000 screaming watts/Blood dripping from my crotch' to the altogether more subtle(!) '90,000 screaming watts/Honey dripping from her pot' reproduced on the album's lyric sheet; the high-paced 'Use It Or Lose It'; 'Save Our Souls', with Mick rekindling his roots on vintage slide guitar before turning

his attentions to an acoustic on the following 'Raise Your Hands To Rock'; while 'Fight For Your Rights' brings matters to a close with Nikki's more serious side coming across clearly in the lyrics.

Without any doubt the record is much more convincing than anything that had gone before, as speedy platinum status proved. As for the group themselves ... well, let's just say that they're more than merely pleased. As Mick told *Kerrang!* journalist Howard Johnson:

'I think this is the best album from the Mötleys so far without any doubt. We've progressed with every LP, but the improvement between this one and *Shout* . . . is larger than the one between *Shout* . . . and the first LP . . . the extra effort we put into it shows up in the grooves. We had more of a budget to play with and more time to get our songs together. We really took our time with the

tunes, sitting down and deciding what direction we wanted to go in.' 'SMOKIN' IN the Boys Room', the first single from the album, came out in the US on June 24 (July 12 in the UK), backed up by a Steve Martin directed video shot in LA, after which the band headed off to Japan for their first Eastern tour (July 7–15) before hitting the road in the States for the first part of a 13/14 month trek taking in every major territory including the UK. All very good news for Nikki, an extended opportunity to do what he likes doing best; playing hard on-stage and partying just as hard in tour bus/hotel or convenient closet once the curtain has descended and the dry-ice diffused.

He now knows when to call a halt, of course, when enough is enough, but that still allows him more than enough leeway to feast and feast again on any female flesh flaunting

itself in his direction, each participating partner apparently required to leave a suitable souvenir item for the band's tour bus (by the end of the Ozzy expedition, the smell in said vehicle was, by all accounts, quite overpowering!). Indeed, in the name of honour and decency, Sharon Osbourne, Ozzy's wife and manager, eventually felt obliged to stop the Crüe bringing any girls backstage, having found them taking photos of a particularly, uh, athletic group in their dressing room bathroom.

And then again, perhaps this time around it'll all be very different. After all, in *Circus* magazine (March 31 1984) Rich Fisher confessed to Richard Hogan that the Mötley gang were really 'angels', anything in fact except the bad boys of rock'n'roll.

'They're in bed by 11 o'clock with their milk and cookies,' he revealed.

Yeah, sure Rich, whatever you say.